Antiques ❧
Illustrated & Priced

Antiques

Illustrated & Priced

Dated and Appraised for the
Collector, Dealer and Decorator

Norman Hudson

South Brunswick and New York: A. S. Barnes and Company
London: Thomas Yoseloff Ltd.

© 1978 by A. S. Barnes and Company, Inc.

A. S. Barnes and Co., Inc.
Cranbury, New Jersey 08512

Thomas Yoseloff Ltd
Magdalen House
136–148 Tooley Street
London SE1 2TT, England

Second Printing 1980

Library of Congress Cataloging in Publication Data

Hudson, William Norman.
    Antiques illustrated and priced.

    1. Antiques—New England—Prices. I. Title.
NK810.H82 1977   745.1′075   76-58584
ISBN 0-498-02109-2

Printed in the United States of America

Contents

Preface

This book is dedicated to that wonderful group of Americana lovers, collectors, decorators and dealers who have become interested in the many and varied items of long ago that have passed from family to family and to friend and for various reasons to the Auction sale.

It is published in the hope that it will help its readers to familiarize themselves with the various types, styles and values of Antique furnishings found in New England.

Each illustration contains four salient features: 1. The actual photograph (*the most critical and important ingredient of any description of an antique item*); 2. A quick word description; 3. The approximate time of its manufacture; 4. The appraised value.

Collectors will discover that a careful comparison of the appraised prices in this 400 page volume with those from the 1972 Edition of *Antiques at Auction* by the same author, shows an interesting trend developing. Some antique pieces are appreciating a good deal more than others and this trend can be charted quite easily.

This updated edition should become a valuable addition to the library of all antique lovers.

Acknowledgements

I am greatly indebted to Richard W. Withington, one of New England's most prominent auctioneers, who made available his vast records and files of past auction material, without which it would have been impossible to produce this book. His help and study of each piece shown and his knowledgeable professional appraisal provides an invaluable guide to the field of fine antiques.

The generous assistance of Daniel Hingston deserves grateful recognition. Without his copious knowledge of antiques, their origin, use and description, I would have been unable to provide the vast amount of valuable descriptive data. "Dan" is truly a walking encyclopedia on the subject of antiques.

Photography by
Robert Swenson
Concord, New Hampshire

Introduction

All of the fine pieces of furniture, lighting devices, the beautiful paintings and prints and other treasured household items illustrated on this volume, were sold at auction in New England by Richard W. Withington from Hillsboro, New Hampshire.

The following few paragraphs, I hope, will get you into the spirit of things as you study the 2,000 illustrations.

It's five minutes before ten o'clock, the two hundred chairs under the tent have long since been reserved by bags of food, knitting, paper signs, an empty carton, a piece of clothing, a neatly tied rope, or the body of the person who will sit attentively for the next six or seven hours.

The caterer has already sold 64 cups of coffee; if the day is chilly, he may have sold twice that many plus a few boxes of pastry and other goodies . . . the audience is at high pitch. Thirty-seven late arrivals are suddenly looking for seats and finding them taken. A sweet little old lady is crawling under a large table, the maker's imprint is being studied on countless plates, pitchers and jugs. Three people are trying to determine the use of the board filled with neatly spaced holes. A stranger to the scene would probably wonder why seven apparently sane people would be looking at the bottom of the drawers from a pretty maple slant top desk, sliding their hands over its side, dumping it over, inspecting its feet, back and hinges, and the stranger would be content to guess that the seven must surely be doctors on a holiday who for the moment forgot the desk is not human. At sixty seconds before ten we find plenty of standees on the circumference of the excitement and from the surrounding area people are hurrying now toward the center of the tent's shelter. Someone says 'what are we waiting for'—and on a raised platform you'll find a smiling face industriously sizing up the attendance, because no one at this particular moment has more interest in who's among the crowd than Richard W. Withington, "Dick" to his friends.

It's ten o'clock and Dick is calling for attention and quiet. Many times before he has been "King for the Day." His followers seated before him make up as diverse a group as one could find. Doctors, veterinarians, engineers and auto mechanics, restaurateurs and butchers, collectors and dealers all are assembled for a day under the tent.

All right, let's get started, who will make it thirty-five . . . and another of "Dick's" Auctions is underway.

Antiques

Illustrated & Priced

Lowboys, Highboys & Bureaus

Queen Anne walnut lowboy, cut corner top, circa 1750

$5,800.00

Queen Anne curly maple highboy, typical of Connecticut, unusual spiral corner columns, circa 1760–80

$8,700.00

Mahogany inlaid swell front bureau with simple French feet and scrolled apron, circa 1800

$1,200.00

Small Hepplewhite mahogany inlaid sideboard with matched veneer and string inlay, circa 1780

$1,200.00

Chippendale block front chest-on-chest, mahogany, restored bonnet and feet, circa 1760–80

$6,200.00

Choice Chippendale mahogany block-front bureau in untouched condition, note top shaped to conform with blocking in drawers, circa 1750–80

$8,900.00

Small Hepplewhite sideboard, string inlay with original brasses, circa 1780–1800
$1,500.00

Swell front bureau, mahogany with satinwood inlay, circa 1780–1800

$1,300.00

Cherry four drawer bureau with ogee bracket base and thumbnail molded top, circa 1760

$1,800.00

Chippendale maple oxbow bureau with bracket base, circa 1780

$1,600.00

Cherry chest-on-chest with rounded quarter columns and ogee bracket base, circa 1750–80

$4,200.00

Queen Anne mahogany highboy with bonnet top, restored bonnet and legs, circa 1760–80

$5,400.00

Maple graduated four drawer chest with bracket base and thumbnail molded top, circa 1780

$1,100.00

Curly maple five drawer graduated chest with bracket base and molded top, circa 1780

$1,250.00

Early Queen Anne highboy, maple with burled walnut veneered drawer fronts, circa 1720

$7,200.00

Chippendale four drawer chest, walnut, ogee feet, unusual molded top, circa 1760

$1,450.00

*Miniature pine four drawer chest with
original graining 20" high, circa 1800*
$1,800.00

*Small maple chest of five graduated
drawers with bracket base and molded
top, circa 1780*

$1,100.00

*Small Queen Anne slipper foot low boy
in cherry, circa 1720–50*

$4,800.00

*Sheraton four drawer bureau, mahogany
with maple drawer fronts, circa 1800–20*
$500.00

7

Chippendale applewood oxbow chest, with bracket feet and original brasses, circa 1750–80

$1,600.00

Queen Anne cherry three drawer chest on frame with writing slide, circa 1740–60

$1,100.00

Queen Anne cherry highboy with star inlay in top drawer, circa 1750

$7,000.00

Chippendale mahogany oxbow bureau with ogee bracket base, circa 1750–80

$2,200.00

Hepplewhite mahogany Baltimore side-board with serpentine front and fine inlay, circa 1780–1800

$1,500.00

Mahogany sideboard with brass rail and paw feet, circa 1800

$420.00

Cherry chest with six graduated drawers with ogee bracket base and fluted quarter columns, circa 1750–80

$2,000.00

Rare Chippendale mahogany inlaid gentleman's wardrobe in three parts with ogee bracket base, circa 1750–80

$1,200.00

9

*Queen Anne mahogany base to highboy
with excellent shell carving, circa 1750*
$1,800.00

*Sheraton swell-front bureau, fine inlay,
mahogany, circa 1800–20*

$900.00

*Queen Anne maple chest on frame, circa
1750–80*

$2,100.00

Queen Anne maple highboy, circa 1750
$4,400.00

French provincial fruitwood bureau, circa 1780

$1,100.00

Sheraton cherry four drawer bureau with rare whalebone drawer pulls, circa 1815
$600.00

Tall curly maple chest of six graduated drawers with molded top and plume carving on bracket base, circa 1750–80
$2,200.00

Graduated six-drawer cherry chest, circa 1780

$1,900.00

11

Hepplewhite mahogany serpentine front sideboard, circa 1780

$1,500.00

Six graduated drawer pine chest with old graining, hardware replaced, circa 1780

$2,100.00

Queen Anne birch highboy with five fan carvings, circa 1750
Probably made in Vermont; note high pad feet

$4,200.00

Hepplewhite inlaid mahogany serpentine front sideboard with center drawer containing butlers desk, circa 1780

$1,800.00

Four drawer maple chest with bracket base, top has 3" overhang, circa 1780
$1,900.00

Five drawer curly maple graduated chest with molded top and bracket base, circa 1780

$1,250.00

Hepplewhite mahogany inlaid bow-front bureau, circa 1780–1800

$340.00

Queen Anne walnut lowboy with concave block center drawer, note scrolls on legs, probably Rhode Island, circa 1720–50
$6,500.00

Tall birch chest of six graduated drawers with Queen Anne base and molded top, circa 1760

$2,200.00

Queen Anne curly maple lowboy with fan carving, circa 1750

$4,700.00

Hepplewhite cherry bow-front bureau with French feet—signed J. Feltt

$1,250.00

Baltimore tidewater sideboard, circa 1820

$900.00

Curly maple highboy in untouched condition, hidden document drawer in upper molding, circa 1730–50

$5,500.00

Queen Anne maple highboy, circa 1750
$5,200.00

Queen Anne dressing table, mahogany veneer, circa 1750

$1,200.00

Maple four drawer chest with serpentine top and ogee bracket base, note double fan in apron, circa 1750–60
$8,300.00

Queen Anne maple highboy, circa 1750
$4,800.00

Maple six drawer chest, circa 1780
$1,750.00

Rare Chippendale mahogany scroll-top.
Philadelphia highboy, circa 1750–80
$24,750.00

Maple four drawer chest, circa 1780
$1,100.00

Early Queen Anne highboy, found in
shed with legs cut off, circa 1740
$2,500.00

Curly maple chest-on-chest with ogee bracket base, New England, circa 1760–80

$5,000.00

Curly maple chest-on-chest with ogee bracket base, large fan carving in top and small fan on apron, circa 1760–80

$6,500.00

Maple four drawer chest with molded top, circa 1780

$1,100.00

Chippendale six drawer maple chest, circa 1780

$1,900.00

Hepplewhite maple four drawer chest, circa 1800

$800.00

Cherry four drawer chest with fluted corners and inlaid drawers, base not original, circa 1800

$450.00

Pine two drawer blanket chest made to simulate four drawer chest, circa 1760

$550.00

19

Queen Anne curly maple highboy with fan carving in base, circa 1750

$6,200.00

Four drawer cherry chest with serpentine top, circa 1780

$850.00

a. Liverpool pitchers $200.00

Cherry bow-front bureau with French feet and rare whale bone pulls, circa 1780–1800

$1,000.00

Cherry bow-front bureau with French feet, circa 1780–1800

$1,000.00

Queen Anne cherry highboy, note short legs, circa 1760–75

$7,200.00

Sheraton bureau of birch and birdseye maple, circa 1820

$800.00

Seven drawer cherry chest, brasses replaced, circa 1780

$2,150.00

Queen Anne curly maple highboy, shows no trace of ever having brasses, circa 1750–1780

$5,500.00

Queen Anne lowboy of walnut with Spanish feet, circa 1740–60

$6,400.00

Hepplewhite curly maple four drawer chest, circa 1780–1800

$950.00

Chippendale six drawer chest of curly maple, circa 1780

$2,200.00

Queen Anne walnut lowboy with drake feet, hardware replaced, circa 1780

$7,200.00

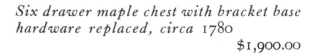

Six drawer maple chest with bracket base hardware replaced, circa 1780

$1,900.00

Chippendale mahogany chest with ogee bracket hase and bow-front, circa 1780–1800

$1,200.00

Queen Anne maple highboy, with bandy legs, circa 1750–70

$6,200.00

Queen Anne pine and maple highboy with oak legs, circa 1760

$2,800.00

Mahogany four drawer chest with French feet, circa 1780–1800

$1,100.00

Hepplewhite mahogany bow-front bureau with pin wheel carving in apron, diamond inlay across top, circa 1780–1800

$1,500.00

Cherry bow front bureau with bracket base, circa 1780

$1,050.00

Queen Anne maple and walnut highboy with original hardware, circa 1740–60

$4,500.00

Chippendale maple chest-on-chest, circa 1780

$3,500.00

Maple chest with four drawers, mahogany and curly maple inlay, circa 1780

$900.00

Chippendale chest-on-chest, wavy birch, circa 1780

$4,200.00

Hepplewhite cherry dressing table with tapered legs, circa 1780–1800

$450.00

Sheraton four drawer chest, maple and mahogany inlaid drawer fronts, circa 1800–1820

$600.00

Chippendale cherry oxbow bureau with ogee bracket base, circa 1760

$2,000.00

Chippendale six drawer graduated maple chest, circa 1780

$2,000.00

Queen Anne curly maple highboy with spliced feet, circa 1740–60

$2,750.00

Chippendale walnut four drawer chest with ogee bracket base and fluted quarter columns, circa 1760–80

$1,150.00

Chippendale mahogany inlaid bureau with serpentine front, note chamfered corners, circa 1760–80

$1,600.00

Seven drawer graduated cherry chest with bracket base and molded top, circa 1760–1780

$2,100.00

Four drawer cherry bureau with loop and tassel inlay at top, French feet and fan inlay in drawer corners, circa 1780–1800

$1,200.00

Hepplewhite mahogany bow-front bureau, circa 1780–1800

$-1,000.00

Sheraton mahogany four drawer bureau, circa 1800–20

$600.00

English, lacquered chest on frame with ball feet, circa 1740–60

$900.00

Sheraton dressing table, mahogany, attributed to Appleton of Salem, circa 1800–1830

$1,600.00

Sheraton mahogany small sideboard, circa 1820–40

$1,000.00

Chippendale maple chest of six graduated drawers, fan carving on top drawer, circa 1780

$2,200.00

Chippendale six drawer graduated chest, cherry, circa 1780

$1,950.00

Mahogany bow-front bureau, feet restored, circa 1780–1800

$1,250.00

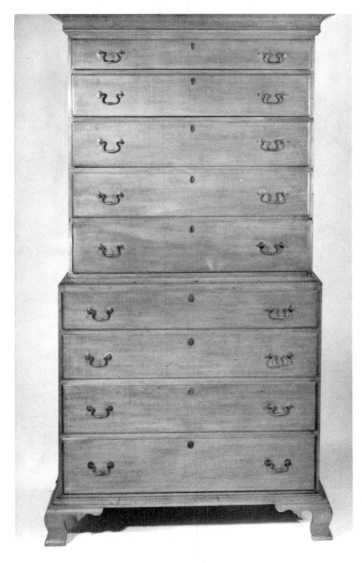

Curly maple five drawer chest, small size with dovetail bracket base, circa 1760–1780

$1,100.00

Chippendale maple chest-on-chest with ogee bracket base and molded top, circa 1760–80

$4,100.00

Maple six drawer graduated chest, circa 1760–80

$1,900.00

Queen Anne curly maple highboy attributed to the Dunlap family, circa 1760
$9,800.00

Chippendale curly maple four drawer chest, circa 1760–80

$850.00

Sheraton mahogany and cherry sideboard with small proportions, circa 1800–20
$1,100.00

Queen Anne cherry highboy base with fan carving, circa 1740–60

$825.00

Queen Anne maple highboy, circa 1740–1760

$3,800.00

Chippendale cherry chest with four graduated drawers and bracket base, circa 1760–80

$900.00

Queen Anne cherry highboy with pineapple carving on top and bottom drawers, circa 1740–60

$3,800.00

Hepplewhite mahogany bow-front bureau with inlay, circa 1780–1800

$1,100.00

Sheraton mahogany sideboard, circa 1800–20

$1,200.00

Hepplewhite mahogany sideboard, circa 1780–1800

$1,800.00

*Queen Anne maple highboy base with
fan carving, circa 1740–60*

$900.00

*Hepplewhite cherry four drawer bureau,
circa 1780–1800*

$875.00

*Maple four drawer chest with bracket
base and molded top, circa 1780*

$1,750.00

*Curly maple six drawer tall chest, circa
1780*

$2,100.00

*Four drawer blanket chest in pine, circa
1760–80*

$800.00

Queen Anne highboy, circa 1740–60
$6,500.00

*Queen Anne English oak lowboy, circa
1740–60*

$900.00

Cherry bow-front bureau, circa 1780
$1,100.00

Mahogany chest with seven drawers, circa 1840

$825.00

Panel front chest, circa 1680–1700
$6,000.00
a. Pewter tankards
$175.00 and $200.00
b. Burl bowl
$450.00

Cherry four drawer bureau, serpentine top, ogee feet, circa 1760–80

$2,100.00

Marquetry inlaid three drawer chest, circa

	$800.00
a. Candelabra	pr. $300.00
b. Tureen	$110.00

Three drawer French Provincial chest

	$1,800.00
Victorian lamp	$125.00
Pair figurines	pr. $110.00

Italian chest elaborately carved

$1,100.00

*English mahogany straight front bureau
with French feet, circa 1800–20*
$925.00

*Base to Queen Anne highboy, circa 1740–
1760*
$900.00

*New Hampshire chest-on-chest attrib-
uted to the Dunlap family, circa 1780*
$7,600.00

*Maple five drawer graduated chest with
bracket base and molded top, circa 1780*
$1,250.00

Hepplewhite mahogany "D" shaped sideboard, circa 1800

$1,400.00

Mahogany bow-front bureau with bracket feet, circa 1800

$1,000.00

Cherry six drawer chest on Queen Anne frame, frame restored, circa 1760–80

$1,200.00

French Marquetry commode with ormolu trim and marble top, circa 1800

$1,500.00

40

*Pine four drawer bureau with painted
and grained ogee bracket base, fluted
quarter columns, circa 1780*

$1,000.00

*Salem four drawer mahogany wood inlay
bureau, circa 1800*

$1,100.00

*Chippendale maple five drawer chest
with bracket base and thumbnail molded
top, circa 1780*

$1,400.00

*Sheraton mahogany Salem server, circa
1820*

$900.00

41

Sheraton mahogany inlaid four drawer bureau, Salem type, circa 1800–20
$875.00

Chippendale cherry four drawer chest with fluted quarter columns and ogee feet, circa 1760–80
$2,000.00

Chippendale maple six drawer chest with dovetail bracket base, circa 1760–80
$1,600.00

Hepplewhite cherry six drawer chest containing a bonnet drawer, circa 1800
$1,400.00

Chests

Pilgrim period panelled and carved oak blanket chest, note initials B. P., circa 1670–1700

$2,000.00

Large oak and pine European sideboard with extensive panelling and carving, 7' 9" long X 39" high, circa 1680

$1,800.00

Pewter pitchers, left & right

pr. $400.00

Two pair of Candlesticks

pr. $150.00

Funnel

$ 40.00

Large deep dish

$400.00

Charger

$150.00

Pair of small porringers

$250.00

Measure

$ 50.00

Pennsylvania dowry chest with three drawers and painted panels, ogee bracket base, dated 1773

$4,200.00

Two drawer pine blanket chest with bracket base, unusual moldings, circa 1760–80

$800.00

Shaker three drawer chest with work table slide, circa 1830

$1,200.00

Connecticut oak four drawer chest with split spindles, circa 1680–1720

$3,200.00

Pine three drawer chest with ball feet, panelled front and sides, circa 1680–1720
$2,100.00

Early tall chest in pine with five graduated drawers and bracket base molded top, old red paint, circa 1760

$1,400.00

Chest of four graduated drawers in old red paint, circa 1790

	$1,100.00
Charger	$150.00
Coffee Pot	$250.00
Coffee Pot	$300.00
Beakers	pr. $ 80.00

Small nine drawer chest, with ball feet, circa 1700

$950.00

46

Thirty-nine drawer apothecary chest with separate cupboard top, circa 1790–1810

$750.00

One drawer blanket chest with ball feet, circa 1700

$2,000.00

New England linen fold chest, circa 1700
$1,900.00

Small English oak ball foot chest, circa 1700

$1,200.00

Pine two drawer blanket chest with bracket base, circa 1700–20

$800.00

Pine two drawer blanket chest, turnip feet, circa 1720

$2,200.00

Small single drawer blanket chest with turnip feet, circa 1720

$1,400.00

Harvard bookcase, made in Vermont, each section lifts off, circa 1820

$900.00

One drawer pine blanket chest with ball feet, circa 1700

$2,000.00

Pine linen fold blanket chest, initials probably those of owner—some scratch carving, circa 1680–1720

$1,100.00

Oak single drawer blanket chest with panel front and pine lid, circa 1700–20

$950.00

Twelve drawer pine spice chest, circa 1830–50

$750.00

Carved oak chest, circa 1700

$1,100.00

49

Single drawer blanket chest, circa 1750
$900.00
a. Pine ball foot Bible box, circa 1720
$650.00

Single drawer pine blanket chest, circa
1720
$1,500.00
a. Slip ware pot $ 90.00
b. Ball foot Bible box $ 425.00
c. Rush light $ 125.00

*Single drawer turned foot blanket chest,
circa* 1720
$3,000.00

Pine linen fold chest dated 1699, *circa*
1700
$1,400.00
a. Hat, circa 1800
$20.00
b. Linsey Woolsey, circa 1820
$300.00
c. Pierced tin lantern, circa 1780
$175.00

a. *Slat back mushroom arm chair, circa* 1720

$1,100.00

b. *Queen Anne looking glass, circa* 1740–60

$300.00

c. *Tin sconces, circa* 1780

each $140.00

d. *Painting of a gentleman, circa* 1820

$650.00

e. *Two drawer pine blanket chest, circa* 1700

$2,100.00

f. *Bannister-back side chair, circa* 1720

$750.00

Five drawer ball foot chest with painted decoration, circa 1700

$2,500.00

a. *Queen Anne mirror, circa* 1720–40

$600.00

b. *Bell bottom candle sticks, circa* 1720

pr. $350.00

Five drawer ball foot chest, pine and maple, circa 1700

$4,300.00

a. Painting of a Lady, done in pastel, circa 1820

$1,400.00

b. Sconce at left $150.00

c. Courting mirror $200.00

Chippendale walnut two drawer blanket chest with ogee feet, circa 1760–80
$950.00

Maple two drawer blanket chest with dovetailed base, circa 1780

$875.00

Single drawer blanket chest with double arch molding, circa 1740–60

$1,050.00

One drawer blanket chest, circa 1680–1700

$2,100.00

a. Bible box, circa 1680

$1,100.00

Chest on frame in single unit, circa 1680

$4,000.00

a. Hanging wall box with drawer, circa 1720

$500.00

b. Pewter porringer   150.00

c. Burl wood bowl   300.00

One drawer blanket chest with ball feet,
circa 1720

$3,000.00

a. *Bennington Pitchers*   Left $240.00
                              Right $250.00
b. *Bennington Bowl* $225.00

English oak dower chest, circa 1740
$1,200.00

Desks & Secretaries

Chippendale mahogany serpentine-front desk with ball and claw feet, circa 1780
$2,800.00

Sheraton mahogany inlaid secretary with cylinder front desk, circa 1830
$2,100.00

Curly maple slant top desk, ogee bracket feet, circa 1780

$3,000.00

*Chippendale maple slant top desk, circa
1780–1800*

$2,300.00

*Small maple slant top desk, circa 1750–
1760*

$3,200.00

*Chippendale cherry secretary with brok-
en arch top and sunburst carvings, circa
1750–80*

$3,300.00

Chippendale ball and claw foot oxbow slant top desk, mahogany, three drawers in bottom section, has unusually high legs, circa 1750–80

$3,200.00

Hepplewhite mahogany secretary with blind doors in top and French feet, original brasses, circa 1780–1800

$1,800.00

Cherry slant top desk, replaced hardware, circa 1780–1800

$2,100.00

Maple slant top desk with Queen Anne feet and sunburst carving, circa 1750

$3,200.00

Chippendale mahogany serpentine front slant top desk with ball and claw feet, circa 1750–80

$2,900.00

Hepplewhite mahogany inlaid secretary with glazed panelled doors, circa 1780–1800

$1,900.00

Hepplewhite mahogany inlaid break front secretary (reputed to be of the family of Eleazer Wheelock, founder of Dartmouth College), circa 1780

$6,000.00

Chippendale slant top cherry desk, circa 1750–80

$2,000.00

Chippendale mahogany serpentine front slant top desk with ogee bracket base, circa 1750–80

$2,700.00

Cherry slant top desk with ogee bracket base and fine interior, circa 1750–80
$2,200.00

36" Maple slant top desk with plain interior, circa 1780

$1,700.00

Chippendale cherry slant top desk with fine interior and ogee bracket base, circa 1750–80

$1,800.00

36″ Maple slant top desk with bracket base, plain interior, circa 1780

$1,650.00

Marquetry desk containing secret well, circa 1760

$1,500.00

Cherry slant top desk with unusual bracket base, circa 1780–1800

$1,800.00

*Chippendale bonnet top oxbow secretary
with ball and claw feet, unusual panelled
doors, circa 1750–80*

$6,200.00

Early pine two drawer desk, circa 1720
$1,450.00
a. Lighting fixture $ 350.00
b. Inkwell $ 110.00

*Hepplewhite mahogany inlaid tambour
desk with French feet, circa 1780–1800*
$1,800.00

Small curly maple slant top desk with fine interior, circa 1760

$2,600.00

Secretary with Vermont graining, knobs not original, circa 1780

$2,000.00

Maple slant top desk hardware not original, circa 1780

$2,200.00

Cherry oxbow slant top desk with ogee bracket base, circa 1770–80

$2,100.00

Chippendale maple secretary with panel doors, circa 1780

$2,000.00

Maple slant top desk, base not original, circa 1780

$1,100.00

Chippendale mahogany serpentine slant top desk with ogee bracket base, circa 1780

$2,150.00

Maple slant top desk with plain interior, circa 1780

$1,400.00

English Chippendale mahogany bombe-front slant top desk, circa 1750–80

$1,350.00

Pine schoolmaster's desk, circa 1800–20

$550.00

Cherry slant top desk, feet replaced, circa 1780

$1,350.00

Birch 36" desk with double step interior, Hardware replaced, circa 1780

$1,750.00

a. Pair of Queen Anne brass candlesticks, circa 1740

pr. $400.00

Hepplewhite mahogany inlaid secretary with French feet, circa 1790–1810

$1,800.00

Chippendale curly maple 34½" desk, 1770–80

$2,600.00

Pilgrim period slant top desk on frame, circa 1700–20

$3,000.00

Curly maple slant top desk with fine interior, circa 1760–80

$2,800.00

Chippendale cherry slant top desk, circa 1780

$1,800.00

Hepplewhite mahogany blind door secretary, circa 1780–1800

$1,150.00

Chippendale mahogany oxbow desk with ball and claw feet, circa 1760–80
$2,550.00

Sheraton mahogany secretary with blind doors, circa 1800–20

$1,350.00

Maple 36″ slant top desk, hardware replaced, circa 1780

$2,000.00

Chippendale mahogany slant top desk, feet have been replaced, circa 1780
$1,100.00

Sheraton mahogany cylinder top desk, circa 1800–20

$1,100.00

Schoolmasters desk on frame, circa 1780–1800

$450.00

a. *Captain's Chair extra high, newly decorated, circa* 1800–20

$140.00

Sheraton secretary, birch and curly maple with heavy legs and carving, circa 1820–1840

$550.00

Chippendale walnut slant top desk, circa 1780

$1,750.00

Chippendale walnut slant top desk with fine interior, shell carving on center door, circa 1760–80

$2,200.00

Hepplewhite, cherry with maple and mahogany inlay secretary, circa 1780

$1,950.00

Hepplewhite mahogany slant top desk, French feet, circa 1780–1800

$1,750.00

Hepplewhite cherry slant top desk, circa 1780–1800

$1,650.00

Shaker ladies desk, circa 1800–60

$1,200.00

Chippendale cherry slant top desk with secretary top, circa 1760–80

$2,200.00

Chippendale mahogany slant top desk with fine blocked interior and four secret drawers, inset shows secret compartments, circa 1760–80

$2,900.00

71

Shaker elders desk, circa 1800–60
$2,900.00

Empire fall front desk, circa 1800–20
$1,000.00

*Hepplewhite mahogany inlaid secretary
with tambour doors, circa 1780–1800*
$2,100.00

Chippendale cherry slant top desk with fan-carved interior, circa 1760–80

$2,250.00

Chippendale birch slant top desk with ogee bracket base and double step interior, circa 1760–80

$2,000.00

Hepplewhite mahogany secretary with blind doors, circa 1780–1800

$1,400.00

Cherry slant top desk with double step interior and dovetail bracket base, circa 1760–80

$1,650.00

*Chippendale maple slant top desk, circa
1760–80*

$2,100.00

*Hepplewhite cherry secretary with
French feet, circa 1780*

$1,900.00

*Chippendale maple slant top desk with
fine interior, circa 1760*

$2,200.00

Chippendale cherry slant top desk, circa 1780

$1,800.00

Pine desk on frame in single unit, circa 1700

$1,300.00

a. *Pewter whale oil lamps, American, circa* 1800–20

$520.00

b. *Book flask, circa* 1850

$300.00

c. *Pewter ink well, circa* 1820

$70.00

Cherry slant top desk with fluted corner columns ogee bracket base, circa 1780

$2,100.00

Fruitwood partners desk, circa 1820

$500.00

Mahogany two part bookcase, circa 1840
$1,000.00

*Marquetry ladies desk with ormolu trim,
circa* 1860

$750.00

*Chippendale desk on ball and claw foot
frame with unique apron, circa* 1760
$4,750.00

Curly maple slant top desk with bracket base, circa 1780

$1,800.00

Fine Chippendale mahogany serpentine-front desk with ogee bracket base and fan carving on apron, block and fan carved interior, original large Chippendale brasses, circa 1760–80

$2,700.00

Cupboards

Pine two part corner cupboard with dentil molding at top and bracket base, circa 1800

$1,500.00

Pine corner cupboard with clover leaf shelves and double panel door, circa 1790
$2,200.00

Pine cupboard, two part, with panelled doors and sides, stile feet, circa 1740
$3,000.00

Walnut and mahogany marquetry inlaid cupboard, circa 1760

$1,100.00

New England pewter cupboard with hooded top, circa 1750

$3,000.00

Formal pine corner cupboard with top cut off, circa 1750

$1,200.00

Pine corner cupboard with clover leaf shelves in as found condition, circa 1750
$1,400.00

Pine pewter dresser, circa 1720

$2,200.00

Two part grained pine cupboard, circa 1820–40

$600.00

*William and Mary hanging cupboard,
English, circa 1700–20*

$620.00

*Pine hutch cupboard with shoe feet and
H hinges, circa 1770*

	$1,500.00
a. Pewter plate	$ 90.00
b. Tea pot	$ 250.00
c. Basin	$ 140.00
d. Basin (down)	$ 110.00
e. Smooth rim plate	$ 135.00

*Chippendale mahogany two part corner
cupboard with H hinges, circa 1780*

$2,000.00

*Dry sink with double breadboard top,
circa 1780*

$350.00

*New England pine dresser, sorry no price
on contents, circa 1760*

$4,000.00

*Pine pewter cupboard with rattail hinges,
circa 1770–80*

$2,800.00

a. Burl bowl, circa 1760

$300.00

*Doctors cupboard, shelf folds down to
writing lid, circa 1780–1800*

$2,200.00

English oak pewter dresser, circa 1740
$1,200.00

Cherry two part corner cupboard with glazed doors and spoon racks, fluted pilaster, circa 1780–1800

$1,500.00

Pine corner cupboard, circa 1780

$1,000.00

Oak panel wall cupboard, circa 1720–40
$350.00

Cupboard base, American oak, circa 1680
$1,500.00
a. *Covered Bible box* $1,200.00
b. *Pair Bennington candle sticks, circa*
1850 pr. $400.00

Chippendale mahogany two drawer linen press, cupboard top and ogee bracket base, circa 1760–80

$975.00

Pine step back cupboard
$950.00
a. *Third shelf on left mocha pitcher*
$225.00
b. *Third shelf on right mocha pitcher*
$200.00
c. *Bottom shelf on right squat bottle*
$225.00

Oriental teakwood curio cabinet
$2,000.00

Pine architectural corner cupboard with glazed doors, circa 1800

$2,050.00

Fruitwood Armoire, circa 1830
$1,750.00

Pewter

Collection of Pewter, limited number of items priced

TOP SHELF: *a. Coffee Pot* $250.00   *b. Pitcher* $300.00   *c. Miniature Queen Anne tea pot* $225.00   *d. Covered water pitcher* $325.00   *e. Coffee pot* $300.00
BOTTOM SHELF: *a. Basin* $200.00   *b. Basin* $200.00   *c. Covered sugar* $220.00
d. Plate behind covered sugar $180.00   *e. Spittoon* $180.00   *f. Swedish dinner pail* $180.00

Collection of Pewter

TOP SHELF: *a.* $75.00   *b.* $30.00   *c.* $30.00   *d.* $55.00   *e.* $20.00   *f.* $35.00
g. $75.00
SECOND SHELF: *a.* $25.00   *b.* $50.00   *c.* $30.00   *d.* $50.00   *e.* $20.00   *f.* $40.00
g. $55.00
THIRD SHELF: *a.* $125.00   *b.* $65.00   *c.* $140.00   *d. pr.* $125.00   *e.* $60.00
BOTTOM SHELF: *Plates a.* $150.00   *b.* $160.00   *c.* $175.00   *d. Candlesticks,*
pr. $225.00   *e. Flagon* $175.00   *f. Mug* $70.00

Collection of Pewter
TOP SHELF: *a.* $60.00   *b.* $30.00   *c.* $60.00 *d.* $40.00   *e.* $60.00
SECOND SHELF: *a.* $25.00   *b.* $25.00   *c.* $30.00   *d.* $50.00   *e.* $30.00   *f.* $25.00
g. $20.00
THIRD SHELF: *a.* $50.00   *b.* $65.00   *c.* $30.00   *d.* $75.00   *e.* $50.00   *f.* $60.00
BOTTOM SHELF: *a.* $90.00   *b.* $60.00   *c.* $65.00   *d.* $65.00   *e.* $80.00

Communion set in pewter, English, circa 1740 $2,200.00

Pewter collection:
TOP SHELF: *each* $50.00
SECOND SHELF: *a.* $50.00   *b.* $50.00   *c.* $150.00   *d.* $60.00   *e.* $60.00
THIRD SHELF: *a.* $75.00   *b.* $50.00   *c.* $125.00   *d.* $90.00   *e.* $75.00   *f.* Pair *of lamps* $260.00
BOTTOM SHELF: *a.* $125.00   *b.* $150.00   *c.* $150.00   *a. Coffee pot* $200.00
b. Coffee pot $225.00

Shelf of pewter
TOP SHELF: *Set of Pewter measures* $350.00   *Porringer* $175.00
CENTER SHELF: *Pewter plate* $60.00   *Plate* $75.00   *Plate* $100.00   *Deep Dish*
$70.00   *Plate* $75.00
BOTTOM SHELF: *Tea Pot* $150.00   *Beaker (Danforth)* $400.00   *Inkwell* $75.00
Candlestick $90.00   *Pitcher (Homan)* $190.00   *Charger* $150.00   *Deep Dish*
$200.00   *Deep Dish* $140.00

TOP ROW: *a.* $200.00   *b.* $150.00   *c.* $80.00   *d.* $55.00
CENTER ROW: $300.00 the set
BOTTOM ROW: *a.* $110.00   *b.* $120.00   *c.* $100.00   *d.* $45.00   *e.* $40.00
f. $125.00

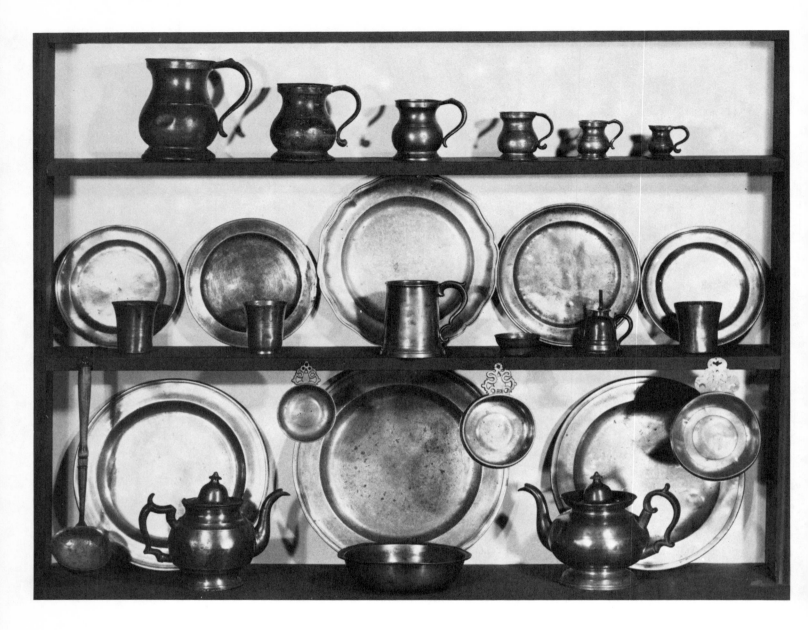

TOP SHELF: *Set of Measures, set* $390.00
CENTER SHELF: *Plates a.* $70.00   *b.* $65.00   *c.* $150.00   *d.* $65.00   *e.* $50.00
Beakers a. $40.00   *b.* $45.00   *c.* $55.00   *Salt* $25.00   *Lamp* $80.00   *Beaker*
$40.00
BOTTOM SHELF: *Plates a.* $160.00   *b.* $190.00   *c.* $180.00   *Ladle* $80.00
Tea Pot $160.00   *Basin* $150.00   *Tea Pot* $175.00   *Porringers a.* $125.00
b. $150.00   *c.* $180.00

TOP SHELF: $250.00 $325.00
MIDDLE SHELF: $225.00 $300.00 $275.00
BOTTOM SHELF: *Plates, each* $ 60.00
              Tea pot $225.00
              Measure $ 40.00
              Tea pot $210.00

Pewter Porringers, circa 1780–1800
a. $180.00   *b.* $175.00   *c.* $975.00   *d.* $220.00   *e.* $240.00
Small Porringers
a. $120.00   *b.* $110.00   *c.* $150.00
Spoons a. $190.00   *b.* $120.00

97

Collection of Pewter

TOP SHELF: *a.–g. Mugs, pr.* $110.00   *b. Plate* $75.00   *c. Mug* $45.00   *d. Deep dish* $150.00   *e. Mug* $45.00   *f. Plate* $50.00

SECOND SHELF: *a.–k. Pair of bull's-eye lamps, each* $350.   *b. Wooden plate* $60.00   *c. Pepper shaker* $22.00   *d. Whale oil lamp* $95.00   *e. Teapot* $225.00 *f. Whale oil lamp* $110.00   *g. Pepper shaker* $30.00   *h. Wooden plate* $60.00

THIRD SHELF: *a. Beaker* $30.00   *b. Creamer* $90.00   *c. Plate* $70.00   *d. Whale oil lamp* $110.00   *e. Coffee Pot* $250.00   *f. Sparking lamp* $100.00   *g. Plate* $55.00   *h. Tea pot* $225.00   *i. Beaker* $35.00   *j. Plate* $45.00

BOTTOM SHELF: *a.–g. Pair of candlesticks, pr* $300.00   *b. Mug* $50.00   *c. Porringer* $125.00   *d. Tea pot* $200.00   *e. Porringer* $110.00   *f. Inkwell* $80.00

Collection of Pewter

TOP SHELF: *a. Whale oil lamp* $140.00 *b. Mug* $45.00 *c. Mug* $35.00 *d. Mug* $40.00 *e. Whale oil lamp* $140.00

SECOND SHELF: *a. Mug* $40.00 *b. Two handled porringer* $120.00 *c. Pepper* $45.00 *d. Whale oil lamp* $120.00 *e. Rare 5⅞" diameter plate marked T. Danforth* $600.00 *f. Whale oil lamp* $90.00 *g. Porringer* $150.00 *h. Mug* $45.00

THIRD SHELF: *a. Mug* $50.00 *b. Plate* $50.00 *c. Beaker* $25.00 *d. Deep dish* $125.00 *e. Inkwell* $60.00 *f. Plate* $50.00 *g. Mug* $60.00

BOTTOM SHELF: *a. Tea Pot* $225.00 *b. Kettle lamp* $100.00 *c. Serving dish* $110.00 *d. Bull's-eye lamp, in tin* $200.00 *e. Coffee Pot* $300.00

TOP SHELF: *a. Wooden scoop* $30.00   *b. Iron Porringer* $45.00   *c. Covered wooden salt* $25.00   *d. Small wooden bowl* $60.00   *e. Butter stamp* $40.00 *f. Iron Porringer* $45.00   *g. Bennington Toby* $40.00

SECOND SHELF: *a. Pewter whale oil lamp* $110.00   *b. Pewter whale oil lamp* $130.00   *c. Pewter mug* $40.00   *d. Wooden pitcher* $50.00   *e. Pewter haystack measures* $75.00, $125.00, $100.00

THIRD SHELF: *a. Chestnut bottle* $80.00   *b. Pewter pitcher* $100.00   *c. Pewter Queen Anne tea pot* $200.00   *d. Pewter spoon holder and spoons* $150.00 *e. Iron rush light* $100.00   *f. Pewter syrup* $50.00

FOURTH SHELF: *a. Pewter candlesticks, pr.* $250.00   *b. Pewter mugs* $25.00 $45.00   *c. Pewter Queen Anne plate* $80.00   *d. Pewter tea pot* $190.00

Mirrors

Eagle convex mirror, gilded, circa 1800–1820

$550.00

One of pair of gilded mirrors, circa 1800
pr. $1,100.00

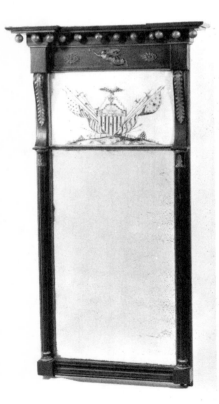

Left—
Sheraton states mirror with reverse painted shield and flag, circa 1820

$350.00

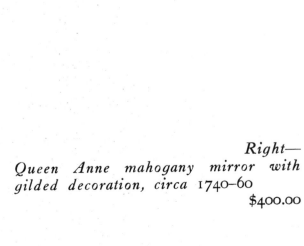

Right—
Queen Anne mahogany mirror with gilded decoration, circa 1740–60

$400.00

Grouping of small mirrors, circa 1700–60
a. $50.00   *b.* $50.00   *c.* $170.00
d. $30.00

Queen Anne mahogany mirror, circa
1720

$1,900.00

Double size Chippendale mirror, circa
1760–80

$2,500.00

103

Queen Anne mirror, circa 1740

$810.00

Chippendale mahogany mirror, circa 1780

$250.00

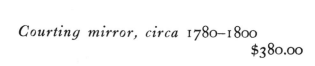
Courting mirror, circa 1780–1800
$380.00

Chippendale mirror with gilded eagle, circa 1750–80

$325.00

Fine Adams style gold leaf mirror with carved basket of fruit, circa 1780–1800
$490.00

105

*Queen Anne mirror with engraved glass,
circa* 1740

$1,100.00

*Queen Anne 46" two part mirror with
applied gold leaf shell, circa* 1740
$3,200.00

*Girandole convex mirror, with candle
sconce, circa* 1800–20

$1,050.00

Convex mirror with eagle, circa 1800–20
$600.00

Sheraton picture mirror, circa 1800–10
$325.00

Hepplewhite gold leaf mirror with baskets of fruit, circa 1780–1800
$550.00

Queen Anne mirror, circa 1740–60
$800.00

a. *Country Queen Anne mirror, circa 1740–60,* $250.00
b. *Country William and Mary mirror, circa 1720–40,* $150.00
c. *Courting mirror, circa 1780–1800,* $320.00

Mahogany Queen Anne mirror, circa
1740–60

$325.00

Chippendale mahogany mirror, 1760–80
$950.00

*Sheraton picture mirror in fine condition,
circa* 1800

$350.00

Sheraton gold leaf mirror, circa 1820
$225.00

111

Chippendale mahogany looking glass, circa 1760–80

$350.00

a. Miniature courting mirror, circa 1780–1800 $500.00

b. Queen Anne painted decoration mirror, circa 1720 $1,275.00

Gilded mirror, circa 1840

$225.00

Chippendale mirror, 1760–80

$500.00

Large wall mirror, circa 1850

$275.00

Salem mirror, circa 1800–20

$325.00

States mirror, gold leaf with cornucopia carving

$250.00

Lighting Devices

Bell metal chandelier, six branches, probably English, circa 1750–80

$950.00

Pewter chandelier, English origin, circa 1800–20

$750.00

Early wrought iron standing lighting device, note brass finial and candle snuffer hook, circa 1750

$750.00

Brass chandelier, six branch with leaf and flower motif, probably English, circa 1780–1800

$650.00

Unusual candle lantern with four candles, circa 1780

$450.00

Collection of lighting devices
a. Pewter bull's-eye lamp $325.00 b. Small onion lantern $160.00 c. Pan lamp with handle $225.00 d. Table rush light $90.00 e. Wrought iron candlestick $145.00

117

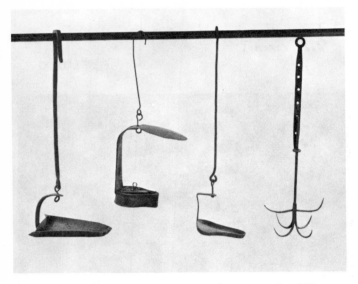

a. *Hanging pan lamp* $60.00   b. *Tin betty lamp* $150.00   c. *Hanging pan lamp* $50.00   d. *Trammel meat hook* $140.00 *circa* 1720–50

Three forms of tin sconces, circa 1780
a. $200.00   b. $290.00   c. $175.00

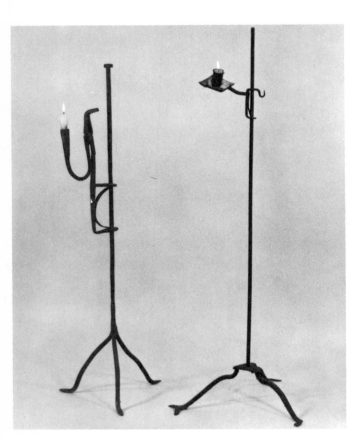

a. *Rush and candle standing wrought iron lighting device, circa* 1740
$425.00
b. *Adjustable candle lighting device, note hook for candle snuffers, circa* 1740
$525.00

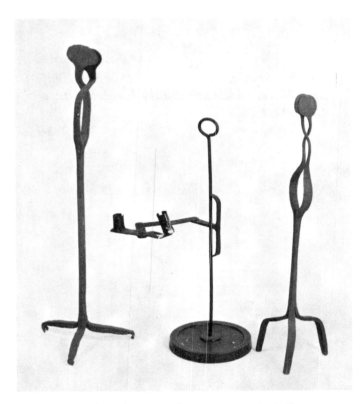

a.–c. *Lighting device for the holding of and burning of burl knots, circa* 1740

each $185.00

b. *Table lighting device with ratchet arm for burning candles, circa* 1740
$325.00

118

Lamp Collection, circa 1740–80
a. Betty lamp and stand $210.00   b. Lard oil lamp, standing or hanging $90.00
c. Tin whale oil lamp with shade $125.00   d. Tin double spout whale lamp $110.00
e. Tin whale oil lamp complete with wick pick $120.00   f. Tin betty lamp with
stand $190.00

a. Tin tinderbox $125.00   b. Tin candle box $110.00   c. Iron pan lamp $100.00
d. Flint striker $50.00   e. Stick end candle holder $55.00
f. Double tin candle lighting device $55.00
circa 1740–80

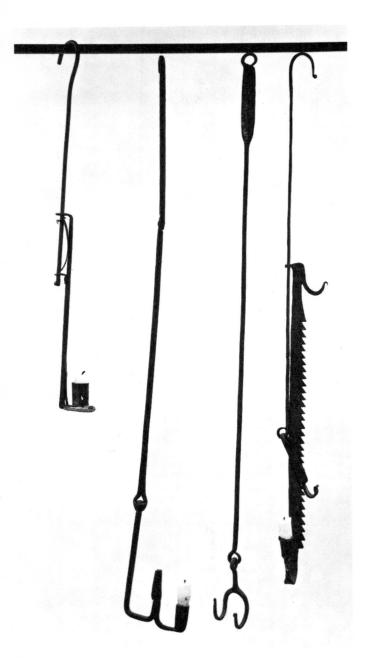

Wood and tin candle lantern, circa 1760
$225.00

a. *Adjustable candle holder* $200.00
b. *Rush and candle holder on swivel*
                                  $380.00
c. *Single chop roaster* $ 65.00
d. *Rachet trammel candle holder* $400.00
   circa 1740–80

Pair of oval tin sconces, circa 1740–60
each $160.00

a. *Screw post candlestand, circa 1720–50*
                                    $800.00
b. *Cross base candlestand with ratchet
   arm, circa 1720–50*
                                    $650.00

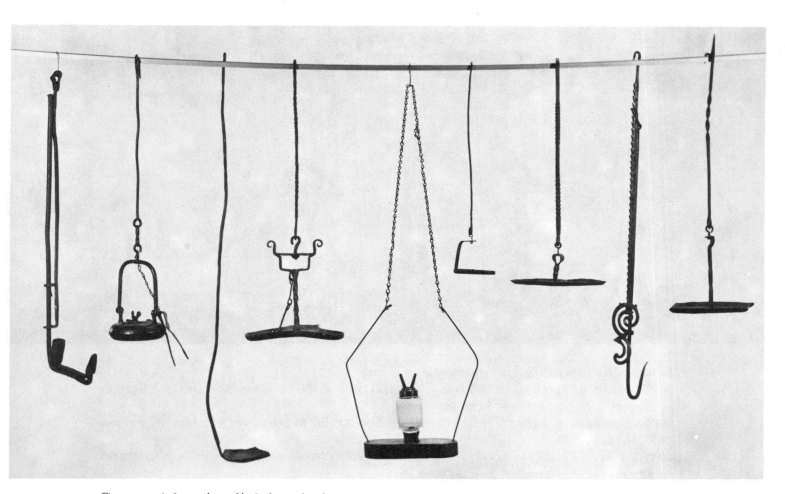

Group of hanging lighting devices
a. $240.00   b. $90.00   c. $85.00   d. $140.00   e. $120.00   f. $90.00   g. $125.00
h. $150.00   i. $110.00

Whale Oil lamps, in tin, pewter, and brass
TOP SHELF: *a.* $90.00   *b.* $90.00   *c.* $100.00   *d.* $65.00   *e.* $110.00   *f.* $90.00
g. $80.00   *h.* $90.00   *i.* $120.00
SECOND SHELF: *a.* $40.00   *b.* $110.00   *c.* $90.00   *d.* $120.00   *e.* $120.00   *f.* $35.00
g. $120.00
BOTTOM SHELF: *a.* $120.00   *b.* $140.00   *c.* $150.00   *d.* $140.00   *e.* $170.00
f. $120.00   *g.* $160.00   *h.* $180.00

122

Pair of Dresden candlesticks

pr. $600.00

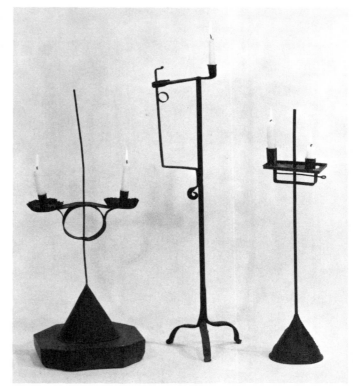

*a. Adjustable table candle holder, circa
1750–80*

$320.00

b. Rush and candle holder, circa 1750–80

$475.00

c. Adjustable double tin candle holder

$340.00

*a. Adjustable table lamp with tin burn-
ers, circa 1750–1800*

$325.00

*b. Pan lamp, for floor or table, circa
1750–1800*

$225.00

*c. Adjustable betty lamp, circa 1750–
1800*

$325.00

*d. Adjustable pan lamp, circa 1750–
1800*

$125.00

Candle lanterns, circa 1750
a. $120.00   *b.* $190.00   *c.* $130.00

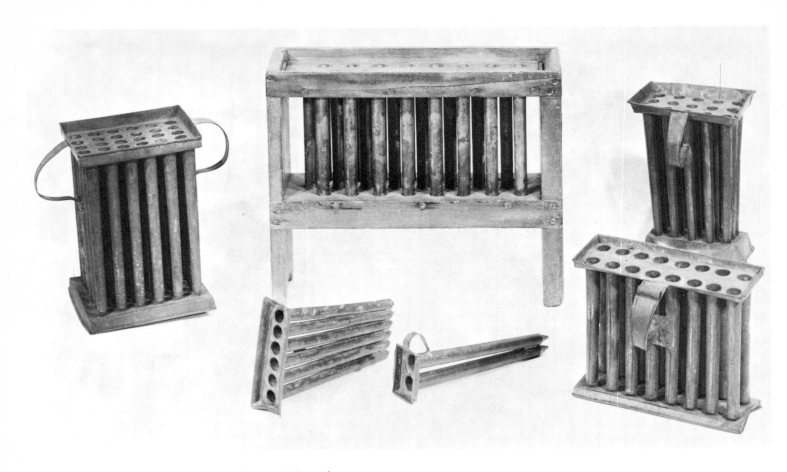

Collection of candle molds, circa 1770
a. $110.00   *b.* $400.00, *wood frame*   *c.* $45.00   *d.* $40.00   *e.* $50.00   *f.* $75.00

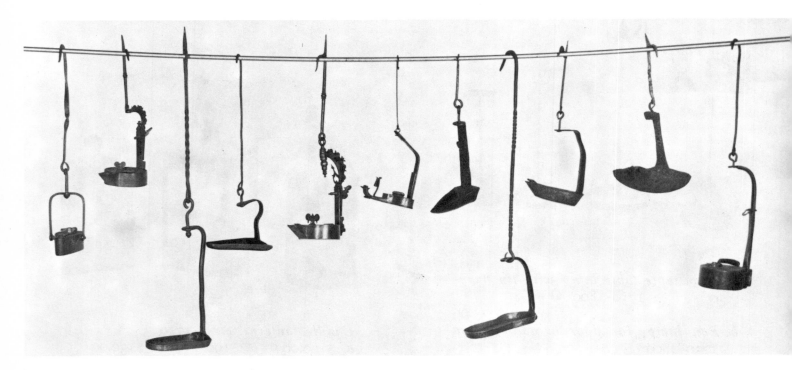

Hanging lighting devices
a. $90.00   *b.* $120.00   *c.* $90.00   *d.* $90.00   *e.* $125.00   *f.* $120.00   *g.* $80.00
h. $150.00   *i.* $130.00   *j.* $160.00   *k.* $100.00

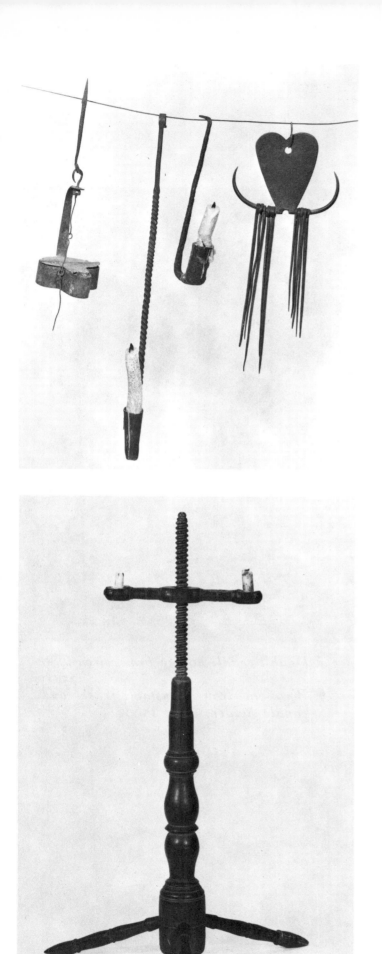

a. *Betty lamp, circa* 1760–80
$100.00

b. *Iron candle holder, circa* 1760
$190.00

c. *Iron candle holder, circa* 1760
$125.00

d. *Skewer holder with skewers, circa* 1760
$575.00

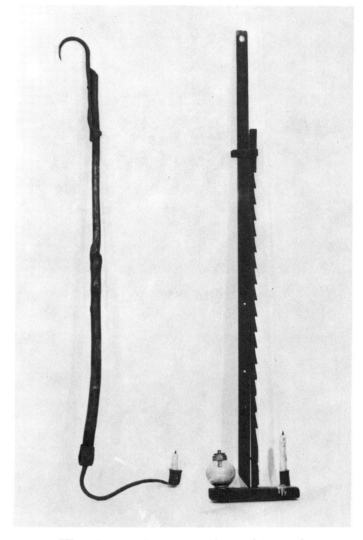

a. *Wood and iron candle holder, circa* 1760
$490.00

b. *Rachet lighting device with peg lamp and candle, circa* 1760–80
$575.00

Screw post candlestand, circa 1760
$1,200.00

125

Four branch brass chandelier, circa 1820
$550.00

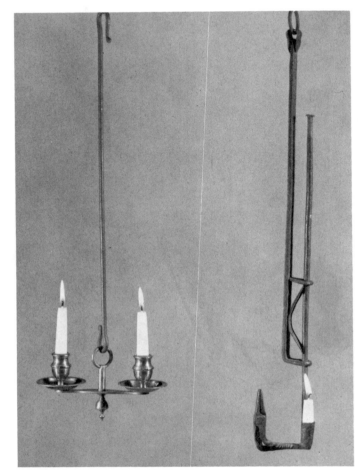

a. Double candle holder, brass, circa 1780
$225.00
*b. Wrought iron adjustable rush and
candle holder, circa* 1760

$275.00

Tin chandelier, circa 1760

$900.00

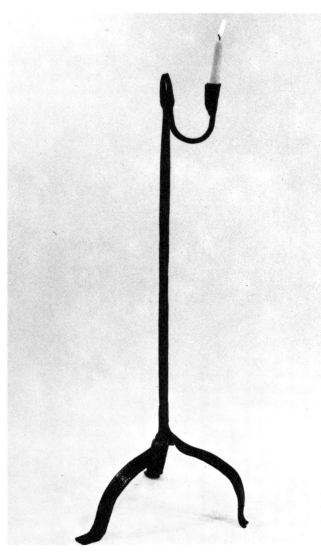

*Three foot standing iron rush light and
candle holder on tripod base, circa 1770*
$275.00

a. *Candlestand* $ 425.00
b. *Rachet lighting device* $1,125.00
c. *Candlestand* $ 725.00
d. *Rush holder* $ 110.00
e. *Betty lamp* $ 100.00

Sandwich glass candlesticks in color and in pairs, circa 1850
a. pr. $250.00   b. pr. $290.00   c. pr. $120.00
(Center:) Canary Whale oil lamps, circa 1850, pr. $700.00

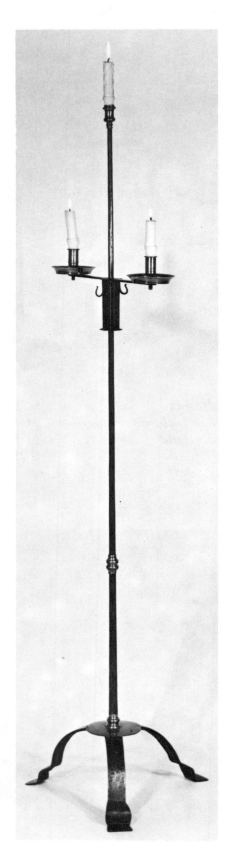

Candle shields 30″ high, oriental gold
leaf decorated and painted paper panels
pr. $400.00

Rare brass and iron floor lighting device
$7,800.00

128

Collection of candle molds
a. $90.00 b. $85.00 c. $50.00 d. $50.00
e. $65.00 f. $45.00, circa 1790–1800

Collection of Lanterns
a. Railroad lantern with whale oil burner
$120.00
b. Candle lantern; Proctersville, Vermont $140.00
c. Pierced tin lantern $ 80.00
d. Candle lantern, painted tin decoration
$120.00
e. Brass presentation lantern, kerosene
$ 90.00

a. Pair rare blue Sandwich glass whale oil lamps, circa 1850 $1,100.00
b. Pair canary Sandwich glass whale oil lamps, circa 1850 $850.00

Decorative glass oil lamps, circa 1850–80
a. $150.00   b. $225.00   c. $550.00
d. $200.00   e. $175.00

Pewter lamps

a. $250.00   b. $200.00
c. $175.00   d. $175.00

Collection of lighting devices, circa 1750–1780
a. *Onion lantern* $200.00
b. *Adjustable candlestick* $325.00
c. *Adjustable double wrought iron pan lamp* $600.00
d. *Pierced tin lantern* $100.00
e. *Footed standing iron candle holder* $275.00
f. *Tin sconce* $125.00
g. *Hanging betty lamp* $120.00

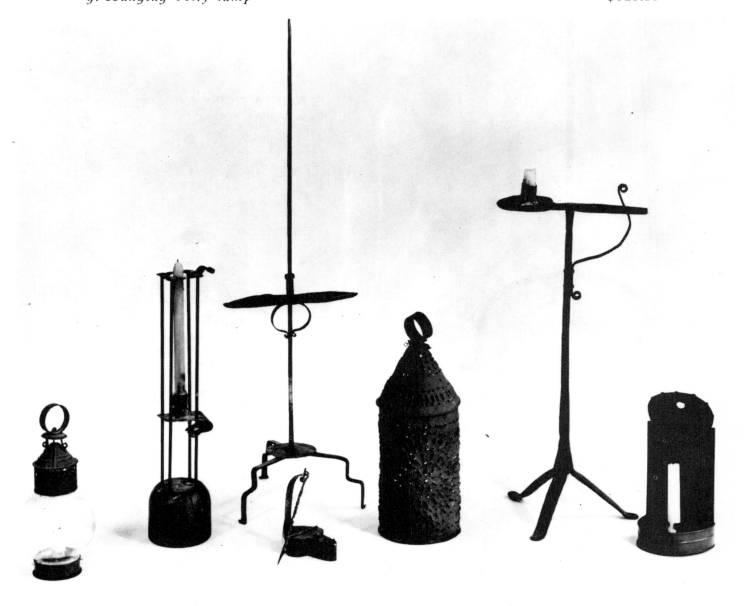

131

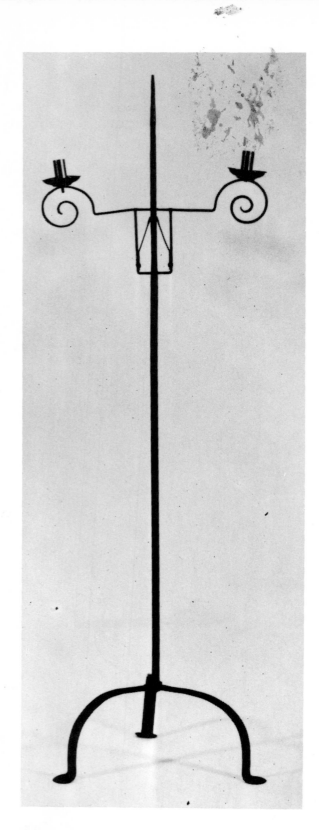

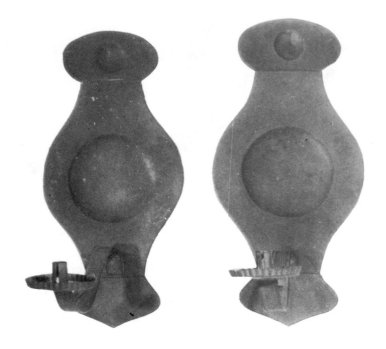

a. Pair rare candle sconces $900.00
b. Tin wall sconce $550.00

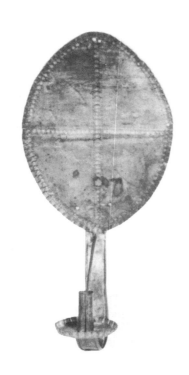

*Twin candle wrought iron adjustable
standing lighting device, circa 1740–1780*
$1,200.00

Pair horseshoe-shaped carriage lamps,
circa 1880 $400.00

Group of sconces, circa 1780–1800
a. Decorative tin sconce for holding rare
  wick lamp $220.00
b. Hanging sconce with snuffer $320.00
c. Pair shaped tin sconces $600.00
d. Pair double candle sconces with raised
  drip pan $1,000.00

Unusual lighting devices
a. *Adjustable spiral candlestick* $190.00
b. *Double tole lamp* $750.00
c. *Iron rush light and candle holder* $110.00
d. *Wrought iron pipe tongs* $600.00

Fireplace Tools
&
Kitchen Utensils

Brass Queen Anne plate warmer, circa 1740–60 $450.00

Pine spoon rack, circa 1780
$250.00
a. Spoons   each $ 15.00

Spoon rack dated 1792
$1,140.00

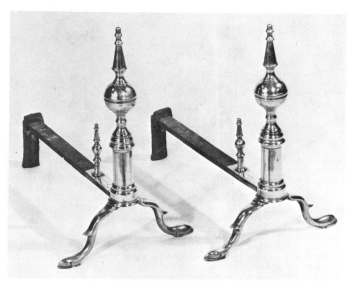

Rare pair of signed andirons by B. Edmunds, Charlestown, circa 1760–80
$700.00

Chippendale brass andirons, circa 1780
$365.00

Rosewood Captain's liquor case (complete), has brass inlay, circa 1830
$525.00

Pair of Chippendale brass andirons, circa 1760–80

$325.00

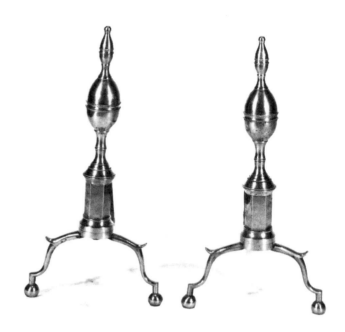

Pair of brass andirons, circa 1780

$310.00

Adam style fire grate, unusual with iron fireback, circa 1840

$635.00

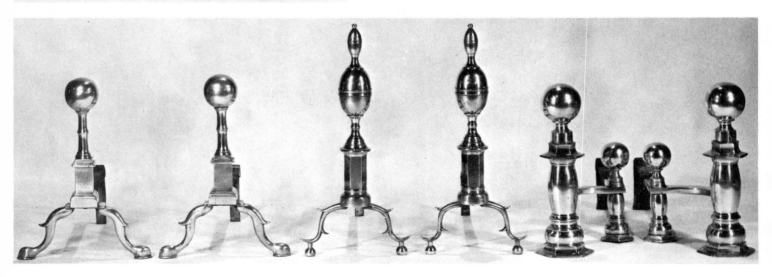

a. Pair Chippendale bell metal and brass andirons, circa 1780, $300.00
b. Double lemon top brass Chippendale andirons, circa 1780, $350.00
c. Pair signed, Hunneman, Boston, brass andirons, circa 1800, $650.00

a. *Foot stool, circa* 1780, $100.00
b. *Foot warmer with carved wood, circa* 1740, $250.00
c. *Wooden piggin, circa* 1780, $ 90.00

Twisted wrought iron toaster, circa 1760
$225.00

a. *Cabbage slicer, circa* 1780

        $ 60.00

b. *Tole tea pot, circa* 1780

     $105.00

a. *Indian mortar* $ 80.00
b. *Wooden chopping bowl with*
 foot $110.00
c. *Wooden scoop with closed*
 handle, circa 1720–40 $ 60.00

Three tier spoon rack dated 1729, probably of Pennsylvania origin

$2,200.00

Small pine hanging shelf with scallop side, circa 1760

$410.00

a. *Pipe box with drawer, circa 1740–80,* $225.00
b. *Candle box, circa 1740–80,* $ 85.00
c. *Candle box, circa 1740–80,* $120.00
d. *Pipe box with drawer, circa 1740–80,* $350.00

Pipe box with drawer and old red paint, circa 1740

$600.00

Adjustable fire screen with drawer, circa 1780 $480.00

a. *Trammel meat hooks* $270.00
b. *Wrought iron meat crown* $225.00
c. *Delicate saw tooth trammel* $150.00
d. *Twisted wrought iron double candle holder* $250.00
circa 1720–50

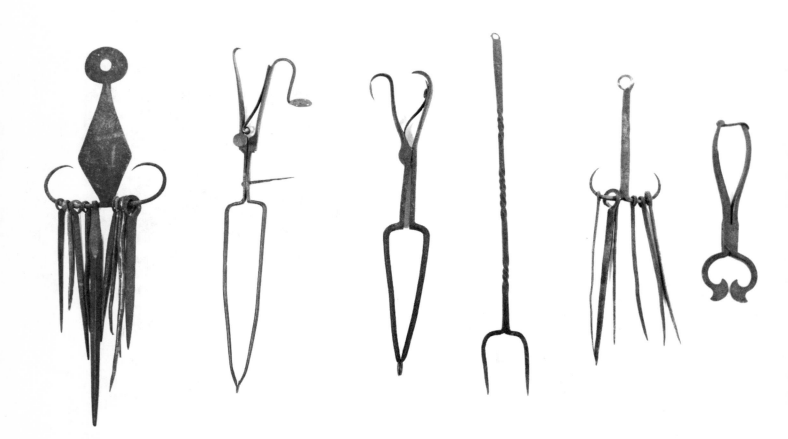

a. *Skewers and holder* $480.00   b. *Wrought iron pipe tongs* $380.00   c. *Wrought iron pipe tongs* $175.00   d. *Wrought iron toasting fork* $55.00   e. *Crude iron skewers and holder* $250.00   f. *Pair of iron sugar cutters* $60.00
circa 1740–80

a. *Milking stool* $110.00   b. *Taper leg stand* $140.00
c. *Churn* $150.00   d. *Tub* $65.00   e. *Oval box* $45.00

Group of wrought iron andirons
a. *Gooseneck design* $325.00   b. *Blade with brass urn top* $550.00
c. *Gooseneck with large penny feet* $250.00

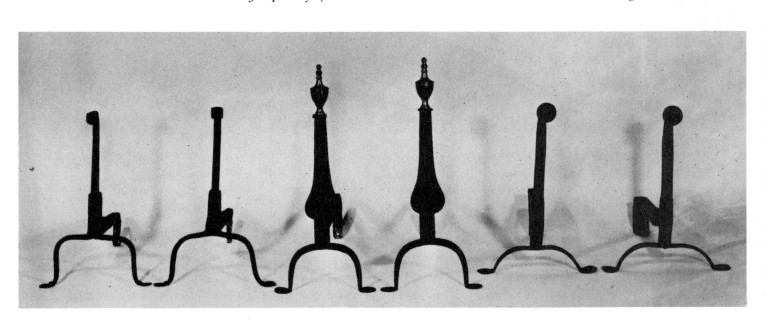

Collection of slipware
Top shelf: a. $300.00   b. $650.00   c. $400.00   d. $400.00
Center shelf: a. $320.00   b. $700.00   c. $100.00   d. $800.00   e. $90.00
Lower shelf: a. $100.00   b. $150.00   c. $80.00   d. $250.00   e. $75.00
f. $300.00   g. $120.00
Early pine panel cupboard with open scalloped top $1,600.00

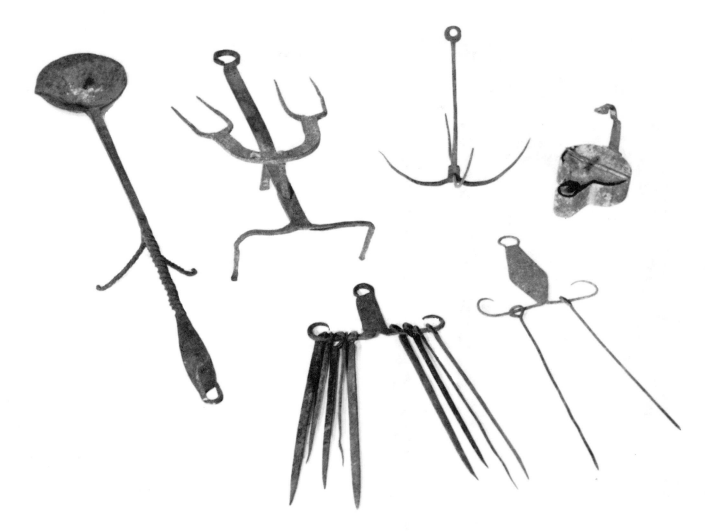

a. Grease ladle $140.00   *b. Toasting fork* $225.00   *c. Grapple hook* $100.00
d. Hanging betty lamp $150.00   *e. Skewers and holder* $325.00   *f. Skewers and holder* $125.00

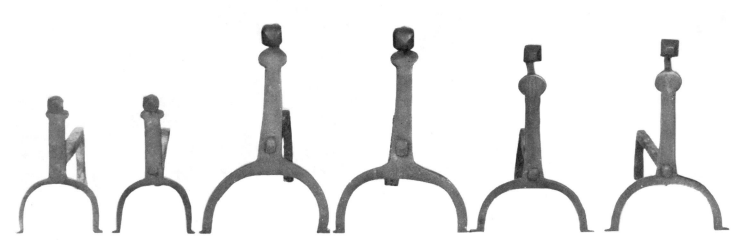

Gooseneck andirons

a. $200.00   b. $325.00   c. $275.00

a. *Candle box* $300.00
b. *Three drawer candle box* $750.00
c. *Double tombstone candle box* $600.00

*Country Queen Anne, pine open cup-
board* $1,625.00
Top shelf: *Mocha mug* $90.00
Mocha bowl $150.00
Mocha tea pot $150.00
Center shelf: *Mocha cup* $60.00
Mocha bowl $240.00
Mocha cup $70.00
*Lower shelf: Oval Shaker boxes, New
Jersey, dated 1830* *Set* $300.00
Large Liverpool ship decorated pitcher
$850.00

Sofas & Settees

Hitchcock settee, circa 1790 $600.00

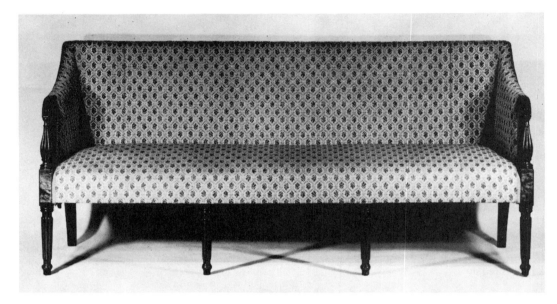

Sheraton mahogany inlaid sofa with six legs, circa 1830 $2,000.00

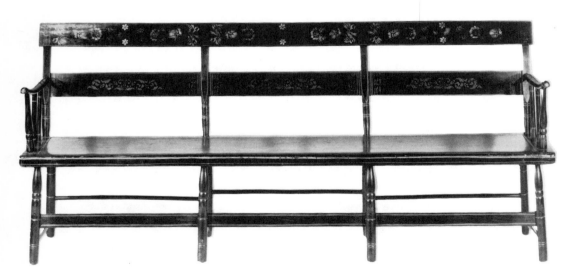

Windsor settee, circa 1820 $475.00

Rare pine child's settle $2,800.00

Windsor "Mammy" rocker $450.00

Victorian carved sofa, circa 1800–30
$700.00

Sheraton sofa in mahogany with eight legs, circa 1820–40

$1,400.00

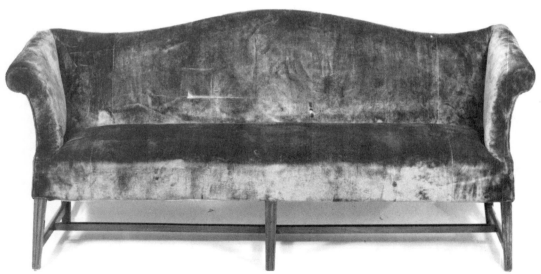

Chippendale mahogany camelback sofa with molded legs and medial stretcher, circa 1780

$1,740.00

Windsor settee with six legs and step down back, circa 1760–80

$900.00

Hepplewhite mahogany eight leg sofa with stretchers and molded legs, circa 1780–1800

$1,550.00

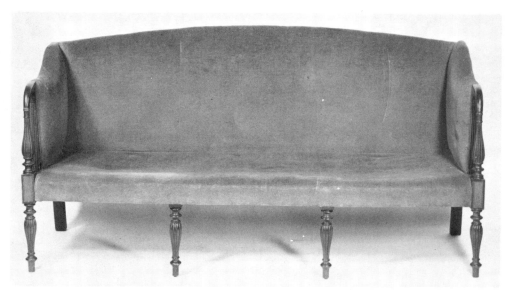

Sheraton mahogany sofa with reeded legs, circa 1820

$1,625.00

151

Marquetry settee, circa 1760

$620.00

Marquetry sofa, circa 1820

$500.00

Chippendale camelback sofa upholstered in needlepoint, circa 1750–80

$2,600.00

Settle bed, Canadian, circa 1700
$810.00

Pine form, circa 1750–60
$225.00

William and Mary day bed with bold turnings, circa 1680–1720
$1,800.00

Sheraton rare mahogany and satinwood sofa of finest proportions, probably Salem —note pineapple carving and detail on arms (in photo at upper right), circa 1800
$6,800.00

Windsor settee, circa 1780–1800
$1,150.00

*Pine curved back settle with shoe feet,
circa 1740–60*

$1,850.00

William and Mary day bed, circa 1700–
1740 $1,750.00

*Closeup of Inlaid arm, acanthus carving,
and reeded legs.*

Sheraton sofa, circa 1800–20

                              $3,650.00

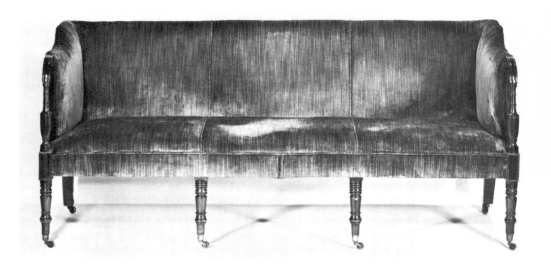

Sheraton sofa, circa 1800–20

$1,400.00

Victorian rose carved love seat, circa 1830

$600.00

Mahogany Sheraton eight leg sofa, circa 1800–20

$1,100.00

Windsor settee, maple, circa 1700
$625.00

Sheraton mahogany sofa with inlay, circa
1820

$990.00

Leather covered Chippendale sofa with camel back and stretcher base, circa 1760–80

$1,950.00

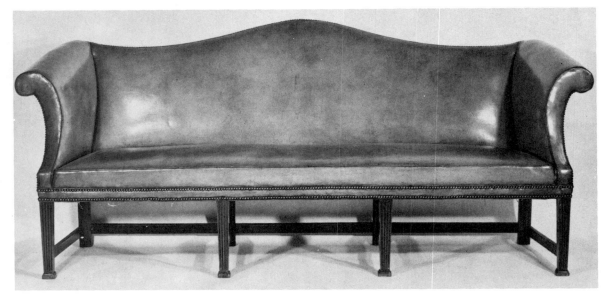

Curly maple Duncan Phyfe cane seated settee, circa 1820

$800.00

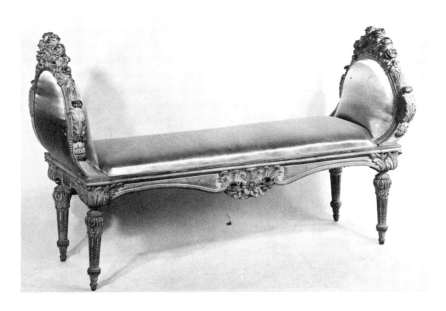

Loveseat, fruitwood, circa 1840–60

$940.00

Sofa with two matching chairs, not shown, teakwood $1,400.00

Queen Anne settee, English, circa 1760–
1780

$1,350.00

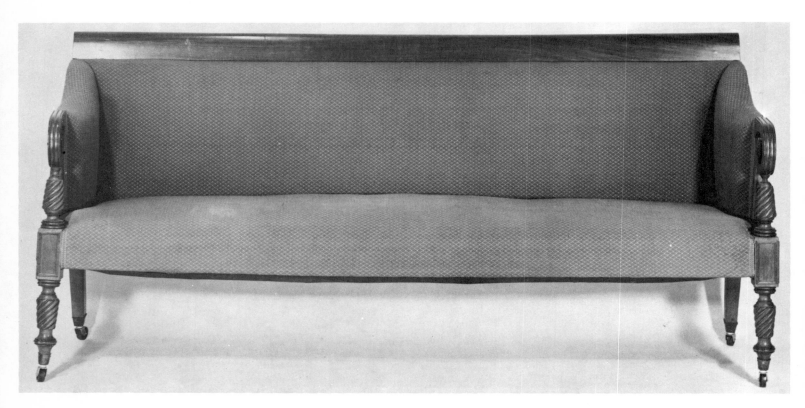

Sheraton mahogany sofa, circa 1820
$810.00

Chairs

a. Pilgrim banister-back side chair with Prince of Wales crest, circa 1680–1720
$1,100.00

b. Oval top tavern table with splayed legs, circa 1680–1720

$1,190.00

c. Banister-back chair with sausage turned stretchers and with plain crest, circa 1680–1720
$610.00

a. Bow-back Windsor rocker with comb-back, circa 1750, $360.00
b. Country Queen Anne arm chair, rocker added at a later date, circa 1700–20
       $425.00

a. *Queen Anne Spanish foot side chair with molded spoon back, circa* 1710–30
$610.00

b. *Small tavern table with shaped apron, circa* 1710–30, $900.00

c. *Country Queen Anne side chair with slip seat and button feet, circa* 1710–30
$580.00

Queen Anne maple side chair with slip seat, circa 1740–60

$1,450.00

a. *Hoopskirt rocker with unusual slat back, circa* 1760

$325.00

b. *Spider leg candle stand with spade feet, circa* 1780–1800

$330.00

a. *Windsor tavern table, circa* 1720–40, $1,260.00
b. *Windsor comb-back armchair, circa* 1760, $ 800.00
c. *Porringer* $120.00
d. *Pewter mug* $ 50.00

165

a. Queen Anne Spanish foot side chair with plain spoon back, circa 1720

$600.00

b. Banister-back side chair with bulbous turning and shaped crest, circa 1720

$325.00

c. Queen Anne yoke-back side chair with original button feet, circa 1720

$340.00

These chairs usually found with bulbous turnings.

a. Four-slat ladder back arm chair with mushroom arms, feet have been extended, circa 1700, $365.00

b. Banister-back armchair with original button feet, circa 1700

$750.00

a. *Ribbon back side chair, circa* 1760, $275.00
b. *Country Queen Anne side chair, circa* 1760, $300.00
c. *Country Chippendale side chair with curly maple splat, circa* 1760, $340.00

Pilgrim century carved childs chair 27"
high, circa 1700

$700.00

Fan-back Windsor high chair, circa 1750–60

$510.00

Single slat 18th century high chair with unique arms, circa 1720

$600.00

Chippendale wing chair with molded legs, circa 1750–80

$1,140.00

169

*Pair Queen Anne Spanish foot side chairs
with molded backs, circa 1710–30*
                              each $690.00

*Hepplewhite mahogany side chair (one
of a set of six), circa 1800*

$300.00

*a. Banister-back armchair with double
   bulbous turnings, circa 1720*

$760.00

*b. Queen Anne Spanish foot arm chair,
   feet restored, circa 1720–50*

$640.00

a. *Queen Anne side chair, 1740–70,* $490.00
b. *Queen Anne maple side chair, 1740–60,* $500.00

Pair of William and Mary side chairs
with cane backs and seats, English, circa
1680–1700

each $380.00

Chippendale wing chair with medial stretcher, circa 1750–80

$1,050.00

Hepplewhite mahogany wing chair, circa 1780–1800

$1,000.00

Rare wainscot chair, circa 1700

$660.00

Chippendale side chairs with slip seats, circa 1750–80, pr. $525.00

Chippendale side chairs, circa 1780
pr. $550.00

Pair of Chippendale maple side chairs, circa 1780

each $340.00

Carver armchair, probably English, circa 1700

$900.00

Queen Anne maple arm chair with Spanish feet, circa 1720

$1,050.00

Double ladderback side chair, circa 1720
$450.00

Pair country Chippendale side chairs, circa 1780

$325.00

a. *Country Queen Anne armchair with button feet, circa 1720*

$1025.00

b. *Early tripod candlestand, circa 1760*

$325.00

Pair of Chippendale mahogany side chairs with pierced diamond shaped splats, circa 1780,   each $525.00

Pair Chippendale mahogany side chairs with pierced splats, circa 1780–1800
each $400.00

a. Banister-back side chair, circa 1740, $300.00
b. Breadboard top tavern table with splay legs and drawer, circa 1720, $980.00
c. Chippendale side chair, circa 1750, $350.00

a Ladderback maple hoopskirt rocker, circa 1750, $280.00
b. Splay leg tavern table with square breadboard top, circa 1740, $775.00

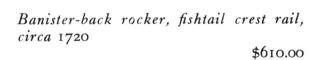

Banister-back rocker, fishtail crest rail, circa 1720

           $610.00

Pair of Rhode Island continuous arm braceback Windsor armchairs, circa 1760
each $690.00

English Queen Anne mahogany corner chair with cross stretcher, circa 1750
$1,050.00

Cromwellian side chair with spiral turnings, circa 1680–1700

$710.00

Carver type high chair, circa 1670–1700
$425.00

Slat-back armchair with mushroom arms,
note large finials, circa 1680–1720
$590.00

Slat-back weavers chair, circa 1620
$275.00

Slat back armchair with unusual mush-room arms, circa 1720–50

$890.00

Pair of Scandinavian side chairs, circa 1700 each $230.00

Pair early ladder back side chairs with unusual top rail, circa 1720

each $260.00

a. Carver side chair with bold finials, circa 1680–1700, $500.00
b. Carver side chair with bold finials, circa 1680–1700, $450.00

Carver armchair, circa 1670-1700
$1,850.00

181

Early oxcart seat, circa 1720–50

$900.00

a. Cromwellian side chair, note shaped stretchers, circa 1680–1720

b. Cromwellian side chair, circa 1680–1720, $525.00
                                                                  $390.00

Early slatback high chair, circa 1720
                                    $340.00
a. Child's rag doll, circa 1820
                         $160.00

Pair banister-back side chairs, note square seat corners, circa 1720–40
each $390.00

Pair Spanish foot Queen Anne side chairs with molded backs, circa 1720
each $910.00

Two early banister-back side chairs of fine quality, note stretchers, circa 1700–20
each $650.00

Pair of early banister-back side chairs, circa 1680–1700
each $710.00

Two maple Queen Anne side chairs, circa, 1740–60

a. $1,200.00
b. $1,070.00

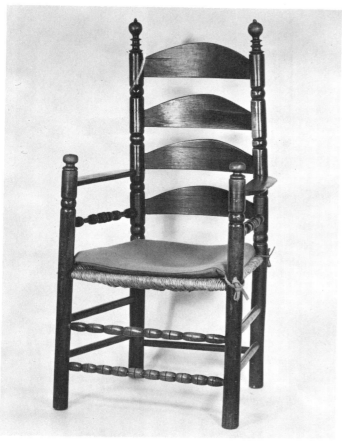

Slat back armchair with mushroom arms and unusual under arm turning and sausage turned front stretchers, circa 1700–20
$1,880.00

Pair of Queen Anne Spanish foot side chairs with molded back, circa 1720
each $920.00

Hepplewhite wing chair, circa 1780–1800, $610.00

Chippendale mahogany carved corner chair with cross stretcher, circa 1780 $500.00

a. Fan-back Windsor side chair, circa 1770, $300.00
b. Splay leg one piece top table, circa 1780–1800, $470.00
c. Fan-back Windsor side chair, circa 1750–70, $320.00

Pair of sausage turned ladder back side chairs, circa 1720

each $325.00

a. Oval top tavern table, circa 1750

$875.00

English Chippendale mahogany wing chair, circa 1750–80

$900.00

Chippendale wing chair, circa 1780

$1,350.00

Left
Comb-back Windsor armchair, circa 1750–80, $345.00
Center
Bow-back Windsor armchair, circa 1750–80, $420.00
Right
Banister-back armchair, circa 1750–80, $850.00

a. Banister-back armchair, circa 1740
$1,075.00
b. Cross-base screw post candlestand,
circa 1750–80

$425.00

Comb-back Windsor armchair, circa
1770

$675.00

a. Fan-back Windsor side chair, circa
   1760 $400.00
b. Fan-back Windsor side chair, circa
   1760 $420.00

*a. Country Queen Anne side chair, note
molded side stretchers, circa 1740–60
$950.00
b. Transitional side chair, circa 1750–80
$510.00*

*a. Banister-back side chair with fishtail
crest, circa 1740–60
$475.00
b. Banister-back side chair, circa 1740–
1760
$450.00*

*Pair Chippendale ribbon-back side
chairs, circa 1780–1800
pr. $720.00*

a., c. Pair of banister-back side chairs with fishtail crests, pr. $860.00
b. Banister-back armchair with fishtail crest, $770.00

Country Queen Anne side chairs with yoke backs, circa 1760

a. $475.00
b. $445.00

Bowback Windsor armchair, circa 1760–1780

$770.00

Sheraton mahogany wing chair, heavy legs, circa 1800–20

$500.00

Queen Anne walnut side chairs with drake feet, circa 1740–60

pr. $2,900.00

Chippendale mahogany corner chair with pierced splats, circa 1760–80

$1,050.00

Banister-back side chairs, circa 1740–60
each $410.00

Banister-back armchair, circa 1760
$710.00

Transition side chairs, circa 1760–80
each $490.00

Sheraton mahogany wing chair, circa
1800–1820   *$500.00*

Two of a set of eight transitional dining chairs, circa 1800

set $2,000.00

Wagon seat with slat back, circa 1800
$500.00

194

a. Country Queen Anne side chair
$475.00

b. Country Queen Anne side chair
$560.00

Banister-back armchair, circa 1760
$700.00

Hepplewhite mahogany side chair with shield back, circa 1780

$300.00

Queen Anne side chairs, Chinese lacquer, set of five, circa 1760

set $900.00

Banister-back armchair with carved crest rail, circa 1760

$705.00

Sheraton mahogany wing chair, circa 1820

$540.00

Slat-back wagon seat, circa 1770–80

$570.00

Sheraton wing chair with mahogany legs, circa 1800–20

$800.00

*Martha Washington chair, covered with
green linsey woolsey, circa 1760–80*
$1,500.00

a. *Country Queen Anne armchair, maple, circa 1740–60,* $675.00
b. *Banister-back armchair, maple, circa 1730–50,* $830.00
c. *Country Queen Anne armchair, maple, circa 1740–60,* $625.00

Banister-back armchair, circa 1740–60
$1,040.00
a. Candlestand with snake feet, circa 1760
$300.00
b. Capstan candlestick, circa 1720
$180.00

a., c. Carver side chairs, circa 1680–1700,   each $400.00
b. Carver armchair, circa 1680–1700, $2,100.00

a. Slat-back side chair with sausage turnings, circa 1720, $450.00
b. Slat-back armchair with sausage turnings, circa 1720, $525.00
c. Slat-back side chair with sausage turnings, circa 1720, $410.00

Pilgrim slat-back armchair
           $1,180.00
a. Adjustable lighting device with
     small wooden stand, circa 1760
           $825.00

a. *Carver armchair, circa 1680–1700*
$2,900.00

b. *Candlestand, circa 1750*
$160.00

c. *Candlestick*
$210.00

William and Mary side chair with Spanish feet and cane back, circa 1720
$1,100.00

Country Queen Anne side chairs with Spanish feet, circa 1740

each $1,000.00

*Set of six fancy Sheraton side chairs,
newly decorated, circa 1800–20*
each $150.00

Pair of maple armchairs with salamander slats, circa 1760 pr. $2,400.00

*Pair of banister-back side chairs with
heart and crown crest rail, circa 1720–40*
pr. $1,210.00

*Country Queen Anne armchair with
Spanish feet, circa 1740–60*

$1,200.00

*Curly maple Empire side chairs, circa
1840* pr. $225.00

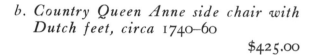

a. *Country Queen Anne side chair with button feet, circa 1750–70*

$300.00

b. *Country Queen Anne side chair with Dutch feet, circa 1740–60*

$425.00

Iron and wood garden bench, circa 1840

$150.00

a. *Banister-back armchair rocker, circa 1740–60*

$300.00

b. *Ladies banister-back armchair rocker, circa 1740–60*

$400.00

Slat-back oxcart seat, circa 1780

$600.00

a., c. Pair bird-cage Windsor side chairs, circa 1780,   pr. $600.00
b. Birdcage Windsor rocker, circa 1780, $225.00

Set of six mahogany shield-back side chairs

each $490.00

Maple slat-back corner chair, good turnings, circa 1760–80

$820.00

a. Windsor bow-back armchair, good turnings, circa 1760, $375.00
b. Windsor high back armchair, good turnings, circa 1760, $650.00
c. Windsor bow-back armchair, good turnings, circa 1760, $600.00

a. Country Chippendale ribbon-back side chair, circa 1760–80

$400.00

b. Chippendale splat back side chair, circa 1760–80

$410.00

Comb back Windsor rocker, circa 1760
$350.00

206

Banister-back maple side chair with button feet, circa 1720–40

$525.00

Transitional mahogany side chair, circa 1770–90

$425.00

Queen Anne maple corner chair, circa 1720–60

$1,100.00

a. Shaker rocker, circa 1800–60

$490.00

b. Shaker rocker, circa 1800–60

$520.00

a. *Shaker slat-back side chair, circa 1800–60*

$250.00

b. *Shaker slat-back side chair, circa 1800–60*

$290.00

c. *Shaker slat-back side chair, circa 1800–60*

$220.00

Country Queen Anne side chairs, circa 1740–60

pr. $1,800.00

Hepplewhite mahogany side chair with shield back, circa 1780–1800

$400.00

Maple comb-back Windsor armchair, circa 1760

$1,100.00

Banister-back armchair with fine proportions, note double bulbous turned stretchers, circa 1720–40

$1,975.00

Set of six English Chippendale side chairs, circa 1780

each $190.00

a. Chippendale cherry side chair with transition back, circa 1780

$200.00

b. Chippendale cherry ribbon-back side chair, circa 1760

$325.00

Chippendale mahogany side chair with carved and pierced splat, circa 1780

$400.00

Sheraton mahogany Martha Washington chair, circa 1800–30

$500.00

Maple Windsor bow-back armchair, circa 1760

$800.00

Pair of country Chippendale ribbon-back side chairs

pr. $390.00

*Set of five Queen Anne side chairs with
slip seats, circa 1740–60*

each $1,180.00

Queen Anne maple side chair with Spanish feet, circa 1740–60

$800.00

Country Queen Anne maple side chair with yoke-back, circa 1740–60

$510.00

Maple bow-back Windsor chair with writing arm and comb-back, circa 1760–1780

$2,300.00

Slat-back armchair with mushroom arms, circa 1760

$510.00

Barrel-back transition wing chair, circa 1800

$900.00

Hepplewhite side chair, circa 1780–1800

$340.00

a. Fan-back Windsor side chair, circa 1760–80

$275.00

b. Bow-back Windsor side chair, circa 1760–80

$260.00

a. Banister-back maple side chair, circa 1740–60

$325.00

b. Country Queen Anne side chair with yoke-back, circa 1740

$375.00

Banister-back side chair, circa 1740
$900.00

*Slat-back armchair with mushroom arms,
circa* 1720

$1,000.00

a. Maple corner chair, circa 1740–60,
b. Windsor writing arm chair, circa 1760,

$875.00
$2,450.00

214

Slat-back armchair, circa 1720

$900.00

a. Tavern table, circa 1740, $1,100.00
b. Hanging pipe box, circa 1740, $ 650.00
c. Wooden pitcher, circa 1760, $ 300.00

a. *Tier table, circa* 1860, $225.00
b. *Victorian armchair, circa* 1820, $990.00
c. *Bristol vase,* $ 75.00
d. *Tea caddy* $150.00

Pair carved Belter-type chairs, circa 1840
pr. $690.00

Pair Flemish-style armchairs
pr. $600.00

a. Windsor armchair, circa 1760, $740.00

b. Slat-back wagon seat, circa 1760, $600.00

Teak chairs with marble insert seats

$650.00 $350.00

Comb-back Windsor armchair with continuous arms, circa 1760–80

$580.00

Bow-back Windsor armchair, circa 1780
$900.00

Windsor comb-back armchair, redecorated, circa 1780

$360.00

Windsor bow-back armchair, circa 1780
$500.00

Comb-back Windsor armchair

$675.00

Slat-back arm chairs

a. $1,100.00   b. $900.00

Chippendale side chair with pierced splat
$500.00
Chippendale side chair with ribbon back
$400.00

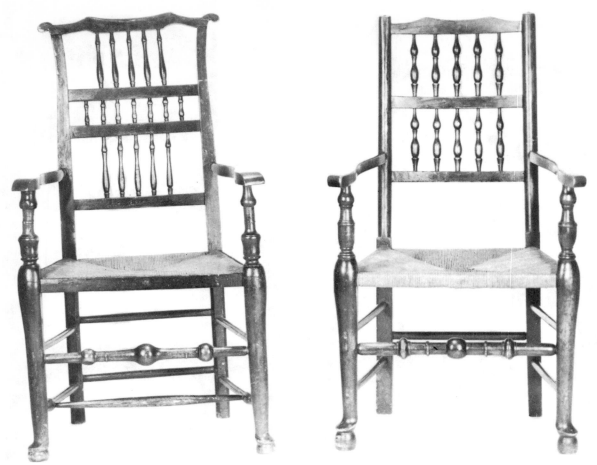

Queen Anne armchairs with rush seats, circa 1750–60　　　a. $425.00　　b. $375.00

a. Birdcage Windsor armchair, circa 1780　　　　　　　　　　$400.00
b. Bow-back Windsor armchair, circa 1760　　　　　　　　　　$600.00
c. Cherry snake foot candlestand, circa 1780　　　　　　　　　$325.00

Delaware Valley ribbon-back armchair with ball feet and bulbous turning, circa
1730–50 $2,500.00

Chippendale mahogany wing chair with stretcher base, circa 1810 $1,200.00

Set of six rush seated Hitchcock chairs in the original decoration $510.00

222

Maple Windsor bow-back armchairs, circa 1760   a. $700.00   b. $600.00

Windsor bow-back armchairs   a. $550.00   b. $500.00

Bird-cage Windsor side chair, circa 1780
$220.00

Bow-back Windsor side chair,
circa 1760–80 $180.00

Windsor armchair with continuous arm,
circa 1760 $750.00

Pair Chinese bamboo chairs   pr. $450.00
a. Mahogany candlestand $275.00
b. Oriental export teapot $175.00

Hepplewhite side chair, circa 1780–1800
$450.00

Comb-back Windsor side chair,
circa 1790 $350.00
Windsor armchair, circa 1800 $330.00

Pair Chippendale side chairs, circa 1780
$700.00 pr.

Pair Queen Anne mahogany side chairs,
circa 1740–60 $1,100.00

Queen Anne mahogany ladies arm chair,
circa 1780 $900.00

Early slat-back oxcart seat, circa 1730
$600.00

Pair stretcher-base coffin stools
pr. $1,000.00

Pilgrim period slat-back armchair,
circa 1700–20 $1,400.00
Primitive tripod candlestand, circa 1760
$900.00
a. Brass candlestick $200.00

Windsor bow-back arm chairs, circa 1780
a. $450.00 b. $650.00

Queen Anne country side chairs with yoke backs, circa 1760 a. $650.00 b. $650.00

Country Queen Anne side chairs with yoke backs, circa 1740–60
a. $300.00 b. $550.00 c. $350.00

227

Fan-back Windsor side chair, circa 1790
$525.00

Queen Anne side chair with slip seat,
circa 1840 $950.00

New York Chippendale side chairs,
a. Pierced splat and carved knees,
    circa 1770 $1,000.00
b. Mahogany arm chair with ball and
    claw feet and shell carving,
    circa 1760–80 $2,500.00

a. Early slat-back armchair with sausage
   turnings, in the old red paint,
   circa 1760–80 $1,050.00
b. Country Queen Anne armchair with
   yoke back, circa 1740 $850.00

Tables & Candle Stands

a. Mahogany spider leg table with spade feet and tip top, circa 1750–80, $400.00
b. Maple snake foot candlestand with cut corner top, circa 1750–80, $350.00
c. Mahogany snake foot tip top table with pad feet and urn turned column, circa 1750–80, $375.00

Mahogany tip and turn table with bird cage support, circa 1750–80

$950.00

Queen Anne mahogany drop-leaf table with shaped apron, round top and cabriole legs, circa 1760

$775.00

Hepplewhite card table with shaped top and fine taper legs, circa 1780–1800

$650.00

Sheraton mahogany serpentine card table, circa 1800–20

$550.00

Two part Sheraton mahogany banquet table, circa 1800–20

$1,150.00

Duncan Phyfe mahogany tambour sewing table, circa 1800

$825.00

Queen Anne maple tea table with scalloped top, circa 1740–60

$4,200.00

*Shoe foot hutch table, Hudson Valley,
circa 1740–50*

$650.00

*Small Queen Anne 26" maple drop-leaf
table with oval top, circa 1740–60*
$2,500.00

*Hepplewhite card table with plain string
inlay, note shaped top, circa 1800*
$700.00
a. *Pair blue front and clamwater base
Sandwich glass lamps, circa 1850*
pr. $500.00
b. *Liverpool pitcher with ship transfer
on side and eagle on front, circa 1800*
$260.00

*Sheraton mahogany server, English, circa
1800–20*

$650.00

Chippendale Pembroke table with serpentine top all around and drop leaves, has pierced cross stretcher and molded legs, circa 1750–80

$710.00

Country pine Hepplewhite deck-top dressing table, circa 1800

$400.00

Pine trestle-foot table with two board 6' 6" top, circa 1700–30

$1,800.00

Oval top tea table with button feet, note splay of legs, circa 1740

$800.00

Early tripod candlestand, circa 1760
$230.00

Hepplewhite mahogany inlaid card table,
circa 1780

$700.00
a. Engraved bell-metal candlesticks,
medial drip pans, circa 1780–1800
pr. $410.00
b. Bowl *$ 85.00*

Single top tavern table with stretcher
base in untouched condition, circa 1720
$1,800.00
a. Folk art rooster, polychrome wood,
circa 1830–40

$220.00

Small oak gate leg trestle foot table,
English origin, circa 1680–1700
$920.00

Chippendale card table with flower pot inlay, figured mahogany, circa 1780
$550.00

Sheraton serpentine-front card table, one of a pair, circa 1800
$800.00
a. *Pair brass Queen Anne candlesticks, circa 1720* $180.00
b. *Bowl* $ 40.00

Drop leaf table with eagle end cut outs, circa 1720–40
$1,350.00
a. *Comb ware platter* $ 540.00

Hudson Valley dish-top tilt table with hex marks, circa 1720–40
$1,500.00

Maple Queen Anne drop leaf table with cabriole legs, circa 1720–50

$950.00

Oval top shoe-foot hutch table, in old red paint, circa 1720–50

$1,200.00

One board tavern-top, single drawer, table with bold turning and medial stretcher, circa 1720–50

$1,475.00

Unusual hourglass table, circa 1750–80
$2,600.00

Hepplewhite cherry Pembroke table with shaped cross stretcher, circa 1780
$650.00

English three-fold card table with two drawers, circa 1750–80
$950.00

Hepplewhite card table, mahogany, circa 1780
$550.00

Queen Anne drop leaf table with hoof feet, circa 1740–60
$650.00

*Mahogany sofa table, Duncan Phyfe,
circa* 1820

$950.00

*Early gate-leg table with Spanish feet,
circa* 1720

$750.00

*Mahogany tip top table with piecrust top
and carved knees, circa* 1750–80

$1,100.00

Small American 28½″ *Queen Anne mahogany drop leaf table, circa* 1720–50

$2,100.00

Yellow decorated dressing table with deck top, circa 1820

$460.00

a. Cherry snake-foot candlestand with cut corners, circa 1750–80

$350.00

b. Hepplewhite spider-leg candlestand with tip top, mahogany, circa 1780–1800

$440.00

Hepplewhite mahogany inlaid card table, circa 1780

$700.00

Rhode Island Queen Anne mahogany drop-leaf table, circa 1740

$1,750.00

Small round tavern table with drawer and stretcher base, circa 1750–70
$700.00

Chippendale mahogany swing-leg dining table with claw and ball feet, circa 1750–1780
$925.00

Sheraton two drawer lightstand, brass pulls, reeded legs, circa 1820
$400.00

Sheraton mahogany corner washstand, circa 1830–40
$300.00

Hepplewhite mahogany card table with drawer, circa 1780–1800

$400.00

Tavern table with H stretcher and bread-board top, circa 1750

$1,200.00

New Jersey Tavern table in cherry with fine shaped apron and double drawers, circa 1760

$800.00

Splay tapered leg lightstand with unusual cutout apron and old graining, circa 1820

$450.00

242

*Early pine gateleg table with bold turned
legs, probably Scandinavian, circa 1750
$1,400.00*

*Shoe foot hutch table with sponge deco-
ration and drawer in base, circa 1720–50
$1,825.00*

*Tavern table, splayed legs and oval top,
circa 1750*

$1,500.00

Pine water bench, circa 1780

$550.00
a. Saddle jug with cover $300.00
b. Slipware milk pan $ 90.00

Early tavern table with breadboard top, circa 1680–1700

$1,200.00

Great pine gateleg table with oval top, probably not American, circa 1720–50

$950.00

Hepplewhite mahogany inlaid card table with unusual urn inlay, circa 1780

$600.00

Oval top maple tavern table, circa 1720–1750

$750.00

Shoe foot trestle hutch table with breadboard top, circa 1720–50

$1,825.00

244

Pine joint stool, circa 1700

$650.00

Mahogany tip top table with piecrust top, circa 1750–80

$950.00

Mahogany dish top tea table with applied shells and drake feet (not American), circa 1720–50

$900.00

Oval top tea table with button feet, circa 1700

$1,100.00

Oak joint stool, English, circa 1700

$325.00

Round top tavern table with drawer, circa 1700–20

$1,300.00

Cross base candle stand with round top, circa 1720

$500.00

Tavern table with H stretcher, bread-board top, drawer missing, circa 1700–20

$1,400.00

*Pine and maple tavern table with bread-
board top and unusual stretcher, circa
1710–30*

$1,100.00

*Two part Hepplewhite dining table, un-
touched condition, circa 1780–1800*

$1,200.00

Round top tavern table, circa 1700–20
$1,150.00

*Sheraton mahogany card table, circa
1820*

$525.00

Snake foot tip top candlestand, fine inlay on top not showing, circa 1750–70

$500.00

Small Queen Anne mahogany table, English, circa 1750

$850.00

Early pine gateleg table with breadboard top, circa 1700–20

$1,200.00

Maple spade foot candlestand, circa 1780–1800

$350.00

*English Queen Anne mahogany tea table
with candle slides, circa 1750*

$1,100.00

a. *Liverpool transfer bowl* $ 360.00
b. *Queen Anne candle sticks* $ 290.00

*Sheraton flaming birch dressing table,
circa 1820*

$550.00

*Hepplewhite mahogany oval top candle
stand with splayed feet, circa 1780–1800*
$275.00

English mahogany tip top table with birdcage support and piecrust shaped top, note knee carving, circa 1775–90
$1,125.00

Queen Anne mahogany drop-leaf table, circa 1750–70
$975.00

Hepplewhite single drawer lightstand with shaped top, circa 1780–1800
$375.00

Sheraton two drawer lightstand with reeded legs, circa 1820
$425.00

*Pine and maple tavern table with drawer,
circa 1750–70*

$800.00

*Oval top tavern table with curly maple
top, circa 1740*

$1,950.00

*Sheraton card table with serpentine top,
circa 1820*

$725.00

*Hepplewhite spider leg candlestand,
maple top, circa 1780–1800*

$325.00

Mahogany drop-leaf table, circa 1750–70
$1,100.00

Sheraton curly maple Pembroke table, circa 1800–20

$700.00

Hepplewhite mahogany card table, circa 1780–1800

$675.00

Mahogany spider leg candlestand with spade feet, circa 1780–1800

$375.00

252

Sheraton serving table with rope turned legs, circa 1800–20

$700.00

Pine and maple tavern table, circa 1760
$950.00

Duncan Phyfe dining table with accordion slide device, circa 1820

$1,300.00

Sheraton mahogany card table with reeded legs, circa 1800–20

$600.00

Hepplewhite English mahogany card table, circa 1780–1800

$550.00

Chippendale tip top table, circa 1760–80
$650.00

Sheraton curly maple lightstand, circa 1800–20

$450.00

Oval top tavern table, circa 1740–60
$1,200.00

Chinese lacquered gaming table with bird cage support, circa 1780–1800
$500.00

254

Queen Anne maple drop leaf table, circa 1750–70

$950.00

Chippendale mahogany tip and turn table, birdcage support with piecrust top, circa 1760–80

$950.00

Hepplewhite candlestand, circa 1780–1800

$350.00

Cherry spider leg candlestand, circa 1780

$325.00

Chippendale mahogany drop leaf table, circa 1760–80

$1,100.00

Hepplewhite mahogany Pembroke table, circa 1800

$550.00

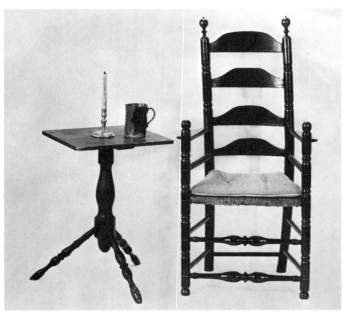

a. Primitive candlestand, circa 1760–80
$300.00

b. Slat back armchair with mushroom arms, circa 1740–60

$750.00

c. Queen Anne candlestick

$125.00

Hepplewhite mahogany inlaid card table, circa 1770–1800

$700.00

Queen Anne tea table, circa 1740–60
$1,400.00

Small sawbuck table, circa 1720–40
$650.00

Gateleg table, circa 1690–1710
$1,200.00

Shoe foot hutch table, circa 1700
$1,460.00

Windsor tavern table, circa 1750
$1,600.00
a. Wooden plates, circa 1740
each $45.00
b. Wooden scoop, circa 1740
$100.00

Gateleg dining table, circa 1690–1710
$1,500.00

a Burl bowl, circa 1740

$560.00

b. Bell bottom candlesticks, circa 1720
pr. $350.00

Queen Anne mahogany drop-leaf table with "C" scrolls on knees, circa 1740–60
$1,400.00

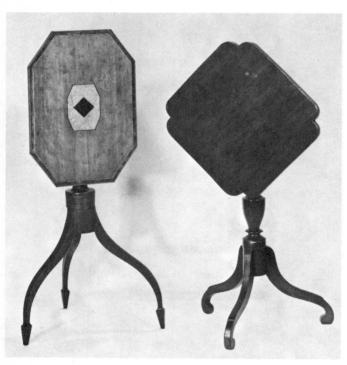

a. Cherry tip top table, inlaid, with spider legs and spade feet, circa 1780
$375.00

b. Mahogany tip top table with cut corners, circa 1800

$350.00

Sheraton mahogany card table with serpentine top, circa 1800–20

$525.00

Mahogany tip top table with bird cage support and dish top, circa 1740–60
$1,500.00

Late Sheraton curly maple serving table, circa 1830–40
$460.00

Pine sawbuck table, top not original, circa 1780
$425.00

Small maple chair-table, circa 1760
$600.00

Hepplewhite country card table, birds-eye maple and cherry, circa 1780–1800
$350.00

Queen Anne maple drop-leaf table, circa 1740–60

$1,450.00

Gateleg table with double gate in back and single gate in front, circa 1780

$925.00

Cherry Pembroke table with bowed stretcher and drawer, circa 1760–80

$875.00

Pine breadboard top table with tapered legs and drawer, circa 1790

$525.00

a. Back Row
Candlemold	$ 60.00
Skating lamp	$ 45.00
Decorated crock made in South Woodstock, Vermont	$600.00
Wooden canteen	$ 40.00
Blown mug	$ 90.00

b. Front Row
Mocha mug	$ 50.00
Brass powder flask	$ 40.00
Betty lamp	$ 75.00
Scrimshaw tooth	$110.00

Hepplewhite mahogany candlestand with shaped top, circa 1780–1800

$310.00

Sheraton mahogany drop-leaf table with drawer, circa 1800–20

$600.00

Duncan Phyfe lyre base card table, circa 1820

$550.00

a. *Mahogany spider leg candlestand, circa 1780,* $350.00
b. *Cherry oval tip top table with spider legs, circa 1780,* $550.00
c. *Cherry candlestand with spider legs and spaded feet, circa 1780,* $500.00

Hepplewhite mahogany card table with curly maple inlay, circa 1780

$1,100.00

Hepplewhite mahogany inlaid lightstand with arched cross stretchers, circa 1770– 1780

$1,750.00

Hepplewhite mahogany card table with inlay, circa 1780

$1,200.00

Hepplewhite cherry inlaid lightstand with shaped top, and heart and string inlay, circa 1780

$825.00

Shaker bedside table with medial shelf, circa 1800–60

$875.00

Hepplewhite mahogany round card table, circa 1780–1800

$500.00

Cherry snake foot candlestand, circa 1760
$400.00

Queen Anne maple drop-leaf table, round corners and cabriole legs, circa 1740–60
$900.00

Queen Anne maple dining-table, circa 1740–60

$1,150.00

Shaker cherry table with single drop-leaf and one drawer, circa 1800–60

$1,200.00

Pair Hepplewhite mahogany inlaid card tables, tops restored, circa 1780–1800

pr. $1,550.00

*Shaker cherry table, one drop leaf and
two drawers, circa* 1800–60

$2,200.00

Shaker single drawer table, circa 1800–
1860

$800.00

*Sheraton two-part cherry dining table,
circa* 1800–20

$1,525.00

Maple candlestand with spider legs and shaped top, circa 1780–1800

$400.00

Mahogany snake foot candlestand, circa 1760

$350.00

Hepplewhite mahogany inlaid card table with "D" shaped top, circa 1780–1800

$900.00

Chippendale mahogany tripod table, dish top and birdcage support, circa 1780

$1,475.00

Mahogany Pembroke table with drawer, circa 1780–1800

$600.00

English Queen Anne mahogany drop-leaf table, circa 1740–60

$750.00

Sheraton mahogany table with sewing bag, circa 1820

$300.00

English Queen Anne mahogany gaming table, circa 1760

$800.00

Country pine half-round table with shaped apron, circa 1780–1800

$525.00

Queen Anne maple drop leaf dining table with straight legs and straight apron, circa 1760

$900.00

Mahogany snake foot tip top table, circa 1760

$575.00

Sheraton cherry country card table, circa 1800–20

$550.00

Maple snake foot table, circa 1760
$450.00

Cherry snake foot candlestand, circa 1760–1780

$325.00

Maple chair-table, circa 1760–80
$875.00

Cherry drop-leaf table with shaped top, circa 1760–80

$400.00

Queen Anne maple drop leaf table with round top and straight legs, circa 1760
$1,100.00

Oak gateleg table with drawer, circa 1740–60

$950.00

Maple candlestand with tip top and spider legs, circa 1780

$425.00

Cherry candlestand, circa 1760–80
$375.00

Trestle table, circa 1680–1700

                         $3,750.00

  a. Burl bowl, circa 1720 $ 660.00

  b. Ladle, circa 1740 $ 90.00

Banister-back side chairs, circa 1740–60
each $260.00

  a. Tavern table, circa 1700–20

                         $1,400.00

  b. Shaving box, circa 1780

                         $ 250.00

  c. Hanging pipe box with drawer, circa 1740

                         $1,250.00

Butterfly table, circa 1700–20

        $1,800.00
 a. Burl bowl $ 700.00
 b. Scoop $ 125.00

Hepplewhite card table, circa 1780–1800
         $600.00

Queen Anne drop-leaf table, circa 1760
      $1,100.00

Maple gateleg table, circa 1700–20
        $1,200.00
a Bennington candle sticks, circa 1850
       pr. $425.00
b. Bennington bowl, circa 1850
        $300.00

Candlestands
a. Tip top with spider legs, circa
1780–1800

$500.00
b. Snake foot candlestand, circa 1760
$400.00
c. Tip top table with spider legs and
spade feet, circa 1780

$625.00

Sheraton mahogany drop-leaf table, circa
1820

$550.00

Gaming table in fruitwood, circa 1840
$550.00

Regency card table with fluted legs
$400.00

Card table, bamboo turned legs, circa
1840 $550.00
a. Oriental charger $325.00

*Sheraton mahogany drop-leaf table with
rope-turned legs, circa* 1820–40
$550.00

Queen Anne English mahogany drop-leaf table with six legs, circa 1760

$975.00

Side table in mahogany with marquetry inlay

$450.00
a. Pair brass candle sticks   pr. $150.00
b. Oriental figurine $200.00

Queen Anne dish-top tea table with unique candle slides, note finely scrolled apron, circa 1740–60

$6,000.00

Hepplewhite mahogany round card table with bell flower inlay, circa 1780

$550.00

Mahogany spider leg candlestand, circa 1780

$330.00

Curly maple button foot country tea table, circa 1760

$650.00

Cherry Pembroke table with drawer, circa 1800

$450.00

Mahogany tip top table with snake feet, circa 1780

$600.00

Queen Anne mahogany English table, circa 1760

$500.00

Unusual candle stand with original red, yellow and blue paint, possibly Spanish, circa 1800

$250.00

Hepplewhite mahogany card table, circa 1780–1800

$500.00

Hepplewhite mahogany inlaid card table, circa 1790–1800

$575.00

a. *Hepplewhite birch candlestand with spider legs and spade feet, circa 1790–1800*

$325.00

b. *Cherry tip top table with serpentine top and snake feet, circa 1760–80*

$525.00

c. *Duncan Phyfe mahogany tip top candle-stand, circa 1800–20*

$350.00

Clocks

Rare mahogany grandfather clock with marked face and original 'Aaron Willard, Junior' label, circa 1820

$8,200.00

Timothy Chandler birch grandfather clock (mark impressed on
saddle) fretwork missing, ogee
bracket base and small carving on
apron, circa 1820

$3,800.00

*Fine Massachusetts shelf clock by S.
Taber, mahogany with satinwood inlay,
circa 1830*

$6,000.00

Cherry case grandfather clock
with quarter columns and ogee
bracket base, brass works, finials
missing, circa 1780

$2,500.00

Unusual pine case grandfather
clock with brass dial, circa 1753
$2,700.00

Mahogany inlaid grandfather
clock, attributed to James Cole,
Rochester, New Hampshire, circa
1812

$4,300.00

Rare maple grandfather clock with brass works by Jonathan Ward, Fryeburg, Maine. (Apprentice to Timothy Chandler), circa 1790

$4,800.00

Flaming birch grandfather clock by Benjamin Morrill, Boscawen, New Hampshire, circa 1810–20
$4,200.00

New Hampshire maple inlay grandfather clock made in Sanbornton, New Hampshire by Elisha Smith, Jr., has gallery top, circa 1800

$4,000.00

Small curly maple grandfather
clock with eight-day movement by
Philip Brown 1815, *Hopkinton,
New Hampshire, circa* 1800
$3,800.00

*New Hampshire mirror clock
with rare eight day brass movement, by A. Chandler, Concord,
New Hampshire, circa* 1810
$2,600.00

*Fine mahogany inlaid grandfather
clock by A. Stowell, Worcester,
with ogee bracket feet circa* 1800–
1820
$3,600.00

*Fancy gold leaf girandole clock, copy of
an original, circa* 1880

$1,500.00

Rare Connecticut acorn clock, circa 1845
$4,200.00

33" Massachusetts shelf clock untouched condition, circa 1790

$5,200.00

Maple grandfather clock with fluted corner columns and brass movement, circa 1810

$2,800.00

Pillar and scroll shelf clock by Seth Thomas, circa 1830

$1,600.00

Mahogany veneer grandfather clock, by Aaron Willard, circa 1800 $8,400.00

*Fine New England cherry grand-
father clock with fluted corner
columns and brass movement,
circa 1800*

$3,200.00

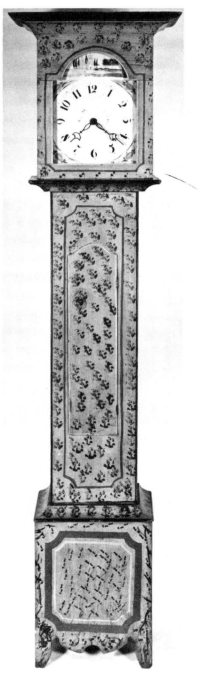

*Grandfather clock with sponge
decoration by Levi Lewis, wooden
works, circa 1809–23*

$5,400.00

*Banjo clock with gold front, circa
1800–20*

$1,500.00

English grandfather clock with brass works, Chinese lacquered case, circa 1760

$2,800.00

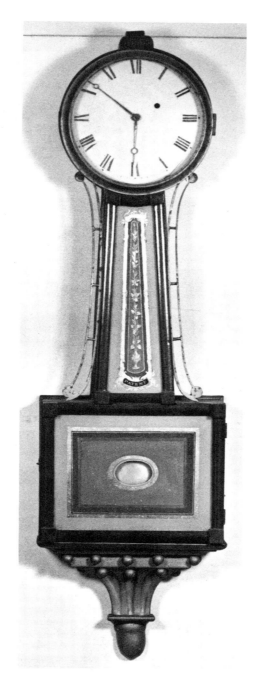

Banjo clock with gilded bracket, circa 1800–20

$1,300.00

Maple grandfather clock with fruitwood top, made by T. Chandler and stamped on saddleboard, circa 1820

$4,200.00

Pillar and scroll shelf clock made by Eli Terry, Jr., circa 1830

$1,450.00

Mahogany inlaid grandfather clock probably New York State, circa 1790–1810

$2,600.00

Mahogany grandfather clock by Nathaniel Mulliken, circa 1780

$5,700.00

*Banjo clock with gold front,
marked Aaron Willard, Jr.
stamped on movement behind
dial, circa 1825*

$3,500.00

*Banjo clock with alarm bell, circa
1820*

$3,200.00

*Chinese lacquered case grand-
father clock, brass works, circa
1760*

$2,600.00

*Pillar and scroll shelf clock by Mark
Levenworth & Co., circa* 1830
$1,650.00

*Banjo clock by Simon Willard and Sons,
mahogany front, wood bezel, circa* 1830
$1,400.00

*N. E. cherry grandfather clock
with brass works, circa 1820*
                $3,200.00

*Pine case grandfather clock by R.
Whiting, circa 1830*

            $2,200.00

*Pillar and scroll shelf clock by Silas
Hoadley, circa 1830*

                        $1,550.00

Mahogany front banjo clock with bracket, circa 1830

$1,300.00

Pine grandfather clock, signed S. Hoadley, circa 1830

$2,100.00

Banjo clock with mahogany front and wood bezel, circa 1830

$1,100.00

Mahogany front banjo clock with wood side arms, circa 1830

$1,250.00

Pillar and scroll shelf clock by Ephraim Downes, circa 1830

$1,750.00

Reeded quarter columns grandfather clock by David Wood, circa 1820

$4,500.00

Clocks, circa 1830,
a. Double decker, carved eagle with reverse painting of Washington on glass
$ 600.00
b. Pillar and scroll shelf clock by Eli and Samuel Terry
$1,200.00
c. Double decker by Daniel Pratt
$ 475.00

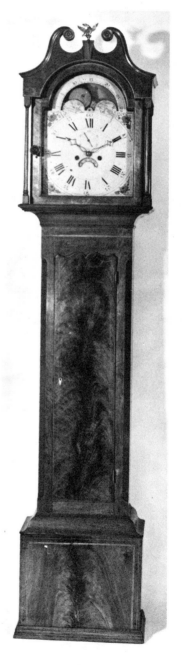

English, pine grandfather clock,
circa 1800–20

$1,400.00

Pine case grandfather clock by
John Hockins, circa 1830
$2,000.00
a. Hat box, circa 1830
$ 110.00

Mahogany grandfather clock with
brass works, circa 1800–20
$1,950.00

a. Massachusetts type pillar and scroll clock by Eli Terry and Sons, circa 1830,

$850.00

b. Jerome Darrow's transition shelf clock with fruit carvings and pineapple finials, circa 1830,

$950.00

a. Howard style banjo clock, circa 1850, $1,100.00
b. Gold front banjo clock, circa 1820, $2,100.00
c. Mahogany front banjo clock, circa 1830, $1,000.00
d. Howard style banjo clock, circa 1850, $1,050.00

Pillar and scroll shelf clock by Eli Terry
and Sons, circa 1830–40

$1,600.00

Cherry grandmothers clock, 50"
high with brass dial, circa 1810–30
$5,400.00

Cherry grandfather clock, fluted
quarter columns, with rare double
scrolled ogee bracket base, made
by Stephen Hasham, circa 1780
$5,800.00

Pillar and scroll shelf clock by Eli and Samuel Terry, circa 1830
$1,750.00

Transition clock by Sylvester Clarke, circa 1830

$750.00

a. Pillar and scroll shelf clock by Eli Terry and Sons, circa 1830

$1,700.00

b. Carved column shelf clock by Atkins Downs, circa 1830 $ 425.00
c. Transition clock by Eli Terry, Jr., circa 1830 $ 650.00

Mahogany grandfather clock by
Alvin Lawrence, Lowell, Massachusetts, circa 1830

$4,000.00

Mahogany lyre banjo clock, circa 1830
$2,700.00

Willard type gold front banjo
clock painted with ship battle and
American shield on glass, circa
1830

$1,800.00

a. Pillar and scroll clock by Seth Thomas, circa 1830,

$1,750.00

b. Transition clock with paw feet by E. and G. W. Bartholomew, circa 1830

$900.00

Acorn clock, side arms missing,
circa 1830

$3,200.00

a. Pillar and scroll shelf clock with Atkins stamped on movement, Mt. Vernon
   painted on glass, circa 1830, $1,100.00
b. Transition clock by Riley Whiting, circa 1830, $ 850.00

Mahogany banjo clock with bracket, circa 1830

$1,100.00

Mahogany banjo clock with mahogany side arms, circa 1830–40

$1,150.00

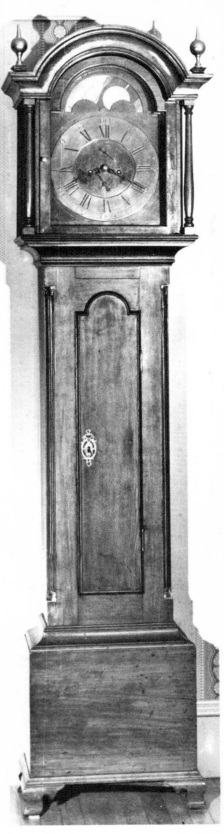

Brass dial grandfather clock by Stephen Hasham, circa 1780

$5,200.00

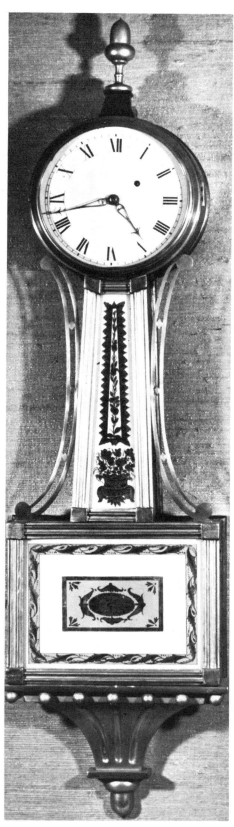

Banjo clock, circa 1820–40
$2,000.00

Scottish grandfather clock, circa 1780
$1,600.00

*Fine Massachusetts shelf clock by Aaron
Willard, has dish dial and painted glass
in top and bottom, circa* 1810

$3,900.00

Triple decker shelf clock with hollow columns, weights run down through the columns, circa 1840

$600.00

Pillar and scroll shelf clock by Jeromes & Darrow, circa 1820–30

$1,400.00

New Hampshire mirror clock, circa 1830
$1,600.00

Grandfather clock with brass dial,
circa 1800

$3,000.00

Grandfather clock by T. Chand-
ler, Concord, N. H., cup finials,
circa 1820–30

$4,300.00

312

a. Mahogany front banjo clock by W. Goodwin, circa 1830

$1,300.00

b. Gold front banjo clock by J. N. Dunning, circa 1820

$1,700.00

Mahogany grandfather clock by John Wilkie, Scotland, circa 1820
$1,900.00

*Rare Tiffany, New York, 13″ shelf clock
with tortoise shell case and ormolu trim*
$1,250.00

*Maple grandfather clock with broken
arch bonnet and brass movement,
circa 1800–30* $2,500.00

Mahogany front banjo clock, circa 1830
$1,200.00

Beds

Sheraton field bed with reeded foot posts and square head posts, circa 1800
$1,050.00

Sheraton canopy top birch bed, circa 1820
$900.00
a. Appliqued quilt, sunburst pattern
$375.00

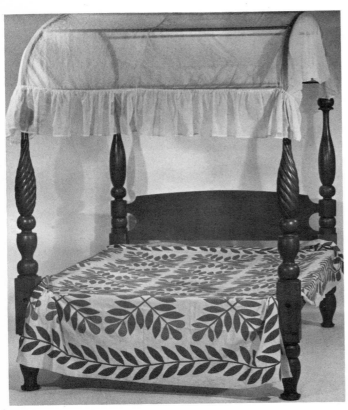

Birch Sheraton canopy top bed, circa 1820 $775.00
a. Appliqued quilt $425.00

Sheraton mahogany canopy bed with heavy posts, circa 1800–20
$850.00
a. Appliqued quilt $400.00

316

Sheraton birch canopy top bed, heavy
posts, circa 1820

$720.00

Coverlet, in chintz $325.00

Sheraton maple canopy top bed, circa
1800–20

$850.00

Birch, canopy top bed, circa 1800–20

$625.00

a. Appliqued quilt, circa 1800–20

$200.00

Sheraton canopy top bed, heavy posts,
circa 1800–20

$600.00

a. Homespun coverlet $275.00

317

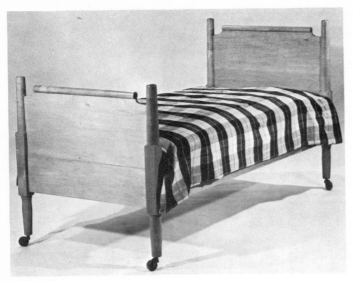

Shaker bed on rollers, circa 1800–60
$950.00

Decorative bed headboard, circa 1840–60
$180.00

Sheraton cherry canopy top bed, circa
1800–20
$850.00

Sheraton birch canopy top bed, circa
1800
$700.00

Sheraton maple canopy top bed, circa
1820
$750.00

318

Paintings
&
Prints

a. Painting on velvet, circa 1860–80, $550.00
b. Painting on velvet, circa 1860–80, $625.00

a. Portrait of English Boy and his dog, circa 1780, $ 950.00
b. Portrait of English Girl holding a flower, circa 1780, $1,000.00

Currier and Ives "Cares of a Family",
circa 1860

$1,300.00

Currier and Ives "Husking", circa 1860
$1,200.00

Pair of Prior Type portraits, circa 1820,   pr. $1,600.00
Courting mirror, circa 1780–1800, $ 450.00

Rare Currier and Ives, large folio
"Home to Thanksgiving", circa 1860
$6,000.00

Primitive landscape painting, artist un-
known, circa 1800

$360.00

Pair of New England primitive ancestral portraits of man and wife, with grained
frames, circa 1830,
pr. $1,800.00

Metford signed full length silhouette, circa 1850

$280.00

Primitive painting, artist unknown, circa 1800

$2,000.00

Rare N. Currier large folio "Camping Out, Some of the Right Sort"

$740.00

Family painting attributed to Negro artist, Joshua Johnson, circa 1800

$6,800.00

Pair primitive animal paintings, circa 1800

$1,100.00

Painting of Indians, unknown artist, circa 1830

$900.00

Painting of Abigail Evans Osgood, Concord, New Hampshire, signed John Brewster and dated April 16, 1823

$1,300.00

Pair of portraits of Deacon Henry C. Buswell and Elizabeth Osgood Buswell, attributed to Cole, circa 1800,

pr. $2,200.00

*Primitive 18th century portrait of Cata-
lina Van Duesen holding roses, artist
unknown, circa 1720–50*

$6,200.00

Pair of ancestral portraits painted by Joseph G. Cole, Dover, New Hampshire, signed and dated, circa 1800,   pr. $2,800.00

Primitive painting of Mehitabel Chloe Buswell, mother of Deacon Buswell, circa 1800

$900.00

327

Painting of gentleman, circa 1800

$500.00

Painting of woman, circa 1820

$450.00

Painting of child, by name of Warren, from Troy, New York, circa 1800–20

$900.00

Portrait of girl holding roses with cat, circa 1800–30

$800.00

Painting of girl with dog, circa 1800–20

$800.00

Full length painting of boy with cart and whip, by an unknown artist, circa 1780–1810

$1,500.00

Ancestral portraits by Zedekiah Belknap, 1781, Weathersfield, Vermont

pr. $3,000.00

Paintings attributed to Prior, circa 1825–70,
a. $850.00
b. $950.00

Stumpwork scene, circa 1700

$700.00

Excellent portrait of young man, circa 1790

$850.00

Painting of lady, circa 1840

$375.00

Still life painting, artist unknown, circa 1820

$550.00

Painting of young gentleman, signed H. Bundy, Claremont, N. H. 1846

$1,100.00

Painting of studious young man, circa 1810

$500.00

Full length painting of brother and sister, circa 1820

$1,600.00

Painting of Richard Gridley, circa 1730–40

$600.00

Profile painting of gentleman, circa 1790

$700.00

Still life painting, circa 1850

$750.00

Painting of girl with pet rabbit, circa 1790

$725.00

Painting of young lady holding flowers, circa 1800

$600.00

Vermont landscape by G. G. Hole, circa 1876

$450.00

Painting of boy with dog, circa 1800–20
$400.00

Primitive painting of horse and farm yard, circa 1850

$575.00

Painting on Velvet, circa 1820–50
$300.00

Jamaica Pond, W. Roxbury, Mass., print, circa 1840

$600.00

Painting of young girl holding two cats, circa 1800–20

$900.00

Pair of portraits attributed to Prior, circa 1825–70, pr. $3,000.00

Painting on academy board, attributed to Prior, circa 1825–70

$300.00

Painting of woman attributed to Prior, circa 1825–70

$300.00

Picture of sailor, painted by a Maine artist, E. E. Finch, circa 1800–20

$440.00

Portrait of woman, circa 1820

$500.00

Portrait of gentleman, circa 1825–50
$440.00

Portrait of grandmother, circa 1800
$325.00

*Painting of a Massachusetts coastal town,
circa 1700–20*

$325.00

Oval portrait of gentleman, circa 1720
$200.00

337

Painting of sisters, circa 1880
$1,100.00

Portrait of gentleman, circa 1760–80
$475.00

Painting on velvet, circa 1840
$780.00

Painting of young gentleman, circa 1780–
1800

$900.00

Still life painting, circa 1840

$850.00

Engraving, printed and sold by Paul Revere, circa 1770–80

$1,200.00

Still life Fruit, circa 1850

$500.00

Painting of boy, circa 1800–20

$550.00

Painting of girl, circa 1820–40

$600.00

Painting of woman, circa 1800

$350.00

Portrait of boy with toy horse, circa 1800
$950.00

Pair of ancestral portraits, circa 1820,   pr. $1,200.00

Fully rigged ship painted by Frank Walton, circa 1820

$1,250.00

Painting of gentleman on wood, by Asahel Powers, Springfield, Vermont, circa 1825

$1,050.00

"The Fox Fanciers," Thomas Kelly

$250.00

Portrait of woman, circa 1830

$400.00

"Trotting Cracks on the Snow," Currier and Ives

$730.00

"A Trot for the Gate Money," Currier and Ives

$425.00

"The End of the Brush," Haskell and Allen

$600.00

"Trotting Cracks on the Brighton Road," Haskell and Allen

$525.00

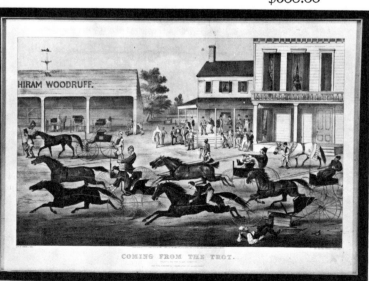

"Coming from the Trot," Currier and Ives

$550.00

343

"Going to the Trot," Currier and Ives

$400.00

"A Brush for the Lead" by Haskell and Allen

$550.00

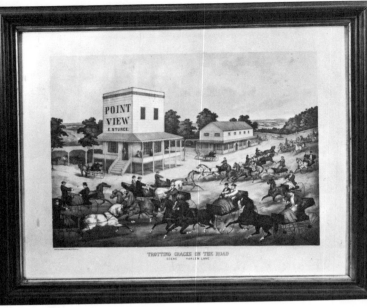

"Trotting Cracks on the Road," Currier and Ives

$500.00

"A Stopping Place on the Road," Currier and Ives

$450.00

"A Disputed Heat," Currier and Ives

$500.00

Portrait of gentleman, circa 1800
$1,100.00

*Painting of Clipper Ship in as found
condition, Andrew Foster*

$2,500.00

Pair of ancestral portraits on canvas, canvas outlined in gold yellow to simulate frame, circa 1800   pr. $4,000.00

Portrait of gentleman with simulated frame in black and brown paint, circa 1800

$900.00

Portrait of James Folsom, born July 8, 1737, circa 1811
a. Inscription on back of portrait

$1,075.00

James Folsom born July 8ᵗʰ 1737. Aged 74 years.

Girl holding pet cat, circa 1820
$650.00

Oil painting, Village scene, circa 1800
$300.00

Pair ancestral portraits, painted 1847
pr. $1,400.00

Ship painting with American flag, circa 1820, $1,800.00

Painting of sisters, circa 1830–50
$825.00

Boy with whip, circa 1830

$625.00

Ancestral portraits, circa 1830–40,   pr. $1,200.00

Painting of child with hat, circa 1840
$750.00

Portrait of woman, circa 1790
$600.00

Still life cat, mouse and cheese, circa 1860–75

$800.00

Portrait of woman holding book, circa 1830

$600.00

Pair ancestral portraits, circa 1840,

pr. $800.00

Ancestral portraits, circa 1830,   pr. $1,500.00

Clipper ship fully rigged, circa 1830
$1,700.00

Pair of oil paintings on wood panels of Dutch landscape, circa 1830–50

pr. $1,000.00

Clipper ship painted by Tudgay, circa
1820

$2,100.00

Painting of two brothers, circa 1840–50
$950.00

Painting of a child with fruit in hat, circa
1830

$650.00

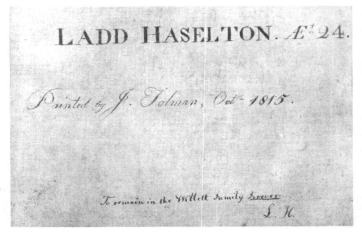

LADD HASELTON. Æ⁴ 24.

Painted by J. Tolman, Octᵣ 1815.

To remain in the Willett Family forever

L. H.

Painting of Ladd Haselton by J. Tolman,
circa 1815

$1,100.00

Painting of girl, Boston label canvas, circa 1830

$450.00

Painting on velvet, circa 1840

$650.00

Painting of trout, by W. M. Brackett, circa 1864

$300.00

Painting of gentleman, circa 1830

$650.00

Painting of Lady, circa 1840–50

$250.00

Painting of girl with hoop, circa 1800

$950.00

Lake "Winnipiseogee", Center Harbor,
New Hampshire, Currier and Ives, circa
1850

$800.00

Painting of girl holding a doll, circa 1840

$750.00

*Water color by Clarine P. Gallup of
Hartland, Vermont, circa* 1850–60

$225.00

Portrait of girl, circa 1830

$450.00

Pair of ancestral portraits, circa 1830,

pr. $1,400.00

Painting of Dutch boy holding a turkey, circa 1760

$300.00

Painting of young boy, circa 1830

$350.00

Painting of child and bird, circa 1830

$800.00

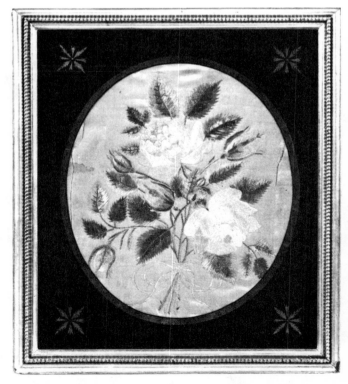

Framed embroidery with Salem, Massachusetts label, circa 1830

$250.00

Ship Lucilla of Boston, bound for China,
circa 1830

$1,450.00

Pair of Paintings by H. Bundy, circa 1847,   pr. $1,900.00

Pair of ancestral portraits, circa 1780–1800,   pr. $1,300.00

Painting of landscape, circa 1840–50
$250.00

Painting of gentleman holding book,
circa 1830–40

$700.00

Painting of ship in distress, circa 1850
$300.00

Painting of Lady, circa 1830

$450.00

Portrait of young gentleman, requiring cleaning, circa 1830

$350.00

Clipper ship "Lightning", circa 1860
$3,900.00

Clipper ship, "Flying Cloud," N. Cur-
rier, circa 1860

$3,900.00

Painting of John Henderson, Esquire,
circa 1816

$550.00

Portrait of Sally Stedman

$7,500.00

Painting of a Lady, circa 1820

$450.00

Portrait of John Quincy Adams Stedman showing back inscription

$7,500.00

Portrait of Jesse Stedman showing back inscription

$7,500.00

*Portrait of Miss Hannah Stedman show-
ing back inscription*

$3,000.00

Oriental hanging

$950.00

*Painting of girl holding flower, circa
1830*

$4,500.00

Painting of Sea Captain holding spy glass, circa 1800–20

$1,100.00

Prior type painting of gentleman, circa 1830

$900.00

Painting of Ship, "City of New York" by Antonio Jacobsen $1,800.00

*Painting of "Ship in Storm" off Thacher
Light, by C. Drew, circa* 1800

$1,450.00

Painting of child with cat, circa 1830

$800.00

Still life painting, circa 1860

$450.00

Ship painting, circa 1850

$850.00

Painting of girl and rose, circa 1830

$450.00

Painting of young girl, circa 1840
$550.00

Currier and Ives, "Camping Out," large folio, circa 1860
$750.00

Portrait of gentleman, Alfred Goodno, Deerfield, Mass., circa 1830
$900.00

Currier and Ives, "Life in the Woods," large folio, circa 1860
$650.00

Miscellaneous China, Earthenware, Export, Soft Paste & Collectables

Marked J. Harris & Son of Boston full bodied Horse, weathervane in copper
$480.00

Long Island folk art wood carved scare crow approximately 42″ high, circa 1830–40

$2,100.00

Tin fish-monger sign, five feet long, circa 1900

$410.00

Pair wood carved Indians, life size, probably not American origin, circa 1780–1800

each $2,200.00

Carved wood cigar store Indian, circa 1820–40

$2,500.00

Carved wood eagle, circa 1760

$800.00

Excellent wood carving of Lady probably used on board ship, circa 1800

$550.00

Iron Indian (repaired), circa 1800

$970.00

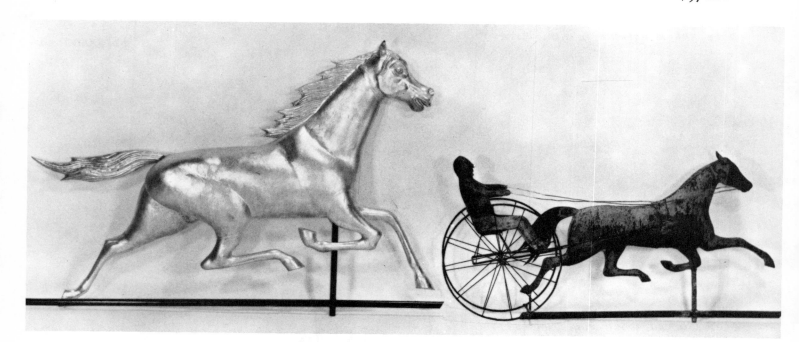

a. Swell-bodied horse weathervane, circa 1820–40,　　　　　$450.00
b. Horse and sulky by L. W. Cushing and Company, Waltham, Mass., circa 1820–40　　　　　$650.00

Sheet metal weathervane, circa 1850
$225.00

*Pair of five foot cast iron garden figures,
circa* 1860

pr. $600.00

Four foot, encased Clipper ship "The Rising Sun", circa 1854, $2,200.00

Toy steam train, tin, steam unit complete, $560.00

Carved wood decoys . . . , each duck $110.00, each goose $275.00

Encased half ship model, Rosewood case, circa 1850–60, $400.00

Collection of Luster Pitchers and Bowls
TOP SHELF: *a.* $75.00   *b.* $60.00   *c.* $110.00
SECOND SHELF: *a.* $60.00   *b.* $50.00   *c.* $65.00
THIRD SHELF: *a.* $70.00   *b.* $80.00   *c.* $70.00
BOTTOM SHELF: *a.* $90.00   *b.* $100.00   *c.* $140.00

Pair rose medallion covered vegetable dishes,   each $350.00

Teakwood curio cabinet

$1,200.00

a. Pair of rose medallion urns
each $1,100.00

Pair of oriental urns with Fu Dog covers
pr. $1,000.00

Three foot bronze incense burner
$600.00

Three pieces of blue Fitzhugh　　　a. $800.00　　b. $225.00　　c. $800.00

378

Lowestoft bowl, 13" in diameter, circa 1760

$1,300.00

a. Interior scene, shows mounted Mandarin warrior

Lowestoft bowl, 12" in diameter, circa 1760

$1,150.00

Rose medallion bowl, 20″ in diameter, circa 1790–1800

$900.00

Collection of Mocha:

BACK ROW		FRONT ROW	
Bowl	$ 90.00	*Pitcher*	$125.00
Pitcher	$125.00	*Pitcher*	$150.00
Commode pot	$ 60.00	*Commode pot*	$ 60.00
Bowl	$ 80.00	*Pitcher*	$110.00
		Cup	$ 75.00
		Cup	$ 90.00

Lowestoft bowl, circa 1780

$550.00

Lowestoft bowl, circa 1780

$725.00

Pair of Chinese export covered urns, circa 1780

pr. $3,200.00

Lowestoft bowl, circa 1780

$650.00

Pair of Chinese export ginger jars with Mandarin figures, circa 1780

pr. $1,200.00

Scrottleware
a. Pitcher $500.00   b. Creamer $325.00   c. Bowl $400.00   d. Marked Bennington
Pitcher and Bowl $700.00   e. Tie backs pr. $80.00   f. Pitcher $225.00   g. Sugar
Bowl $220.00

Bennington
a. Mug $360.00   b. Beaker $75.00   c. Footed beaker $275.00   d. Beaker $200.00
e. Coffee pot $450.00   f. Sugar bowl $250.00   g. Creamer $150.00

Bennington items
  a. Coachman bottles
    1. $325.00   2. $260.00   3. $300.00   4. $350.00
  b. Book flask $180.00   *c. Miniature tea pot* $150.00   *d. Toby tobacco jar* $550.00
  e. Cow creamer $230.00   *f. Tile* $250.00

Pair Venetian wine glasses,   pr. $40.00
a. Compote $90.00   *b. Plates, four* $55.00   *c. Bone dishes, three* $30.00

a. Royal Copenhagen plates,   each $55.00
b. Royal Copenhagen forks,   each $ 7.50

a. Parrot $75.00   *b. Three wine decanters* $50.00   *c. Fruit Compote* $80.00
d. Three leaf plates each $25.00   *e. Cauliflower tureen* $45.00

Four large pottery crocks 18″–24″ *high,* $300.00 $350.00 $650.00 $350.00;
circa 1850–70

Dresden two tier compote

$350.00

Collection of Steins
$780.00 $150.00 $225.00 $115.00 $560.00

TOP SHELF: *Collection of Mocha: a. Pitcher* $180.00 *b. Mug* $100.00 *c. Bowl*
150.00 *d. Pitcher* $200.00 *e. Bowl* $140.00 *f. Mug* $120.00 *g. Pitcher* $300.00
SECOND SHELF: *Collection of Strawberry Soft Paste: circa* 1800
a./g. Pair of plates each $90.00 *b. Plate* $75.00 *c./e. Pair of plates* each $120.00
d. Tea pot $275.00 *f. Plate* $80.00
THIRD SHELF: *Collection of Mocha:*
a. Bowl $125.00 *b. Mug* $80.00 *c./j. Strawberry plates* each $100.00 *d. Pepper*
$110.00 *e. Mug* $140.00 *f. Cup and saucer* $140.00 *g. Large plate, Whieldon*
$250.00 *h. Mug* $120.00 *i. Open salt* $70.00 *k. Mug* $140.00 *l. Bowl* $120.00
m. Mug $80.00

Satsuma vase

$750.00

Collection of Spatterware, circa 1830–40,
TOP SHELF: *a. Sugar with cover, blue* $100.00   *b. Mug, house in color* $80.00
c./d. Twelve piece miniature tea set, in green and pink $180.00   *e. Sugar, green
and blue* $90.00   *f. Cup and saucer, pink* $90.00
SECOND SHELF: *a. Cup and saucer, fort* $95.00   *b./e. Three piece set, peafowl and
green* $450.00   *c. Plate, tulip in green and blue* $100.00   *d. Large cup, peafowl
with pink* $160.00   *f. Butter pat, peafowl* $120.00   *g. Cup and saucer, peafowl
with blue* $130.00
THIRD SHELF: *a. Four blue plates each* $25.00   *b. Cup, primrose with brown*
$60.00   *c. Cup, peafowl* $70.00   *d. Sugar with lid, pink and blue* $160.00   *e. Cup,
rose* $25.00   *f. Cup, schoolhouse* $65.00
BOTTOM SHELF: *a./e. Pair of plates, brown borders and blue cornflower* each
$130.00   *b. Cup and saucer, blue and pink* $160.00   *c. Serving dish, blue border
with green and pink sprig* $225.00   *d. Cream pitcher, blue with tulip* $130.00

Collection of Mocha, circa 1820–40

TOP SHELF: *a. Mug* $90.00   *b. Covered cup* $80.00   *c. Mug* $60.00   *d. Cup and Saucer* $60.00   *e. Mug* $70.00   *f. Sugar* $90.00

SECOND SHELF: *a. Covered cup* $110.00   *b. Mug* $170.00   *c. Bowl* $80.00   *d. Mug* $150.00   *e. Footed salt* $60.00

THIRD SHELF: *a. Mug* $130.00   *b. Mug* $140.00   *c. Mug* $130.00   *d. Bowl* $80.00   *e. Small mug* $40.00

BOTTOM SHELF: *a. Bowl* $90.00   *b. Pitcher* $140.00   *c. Pitcher* $180.00   *d. Pitcher* $165.00

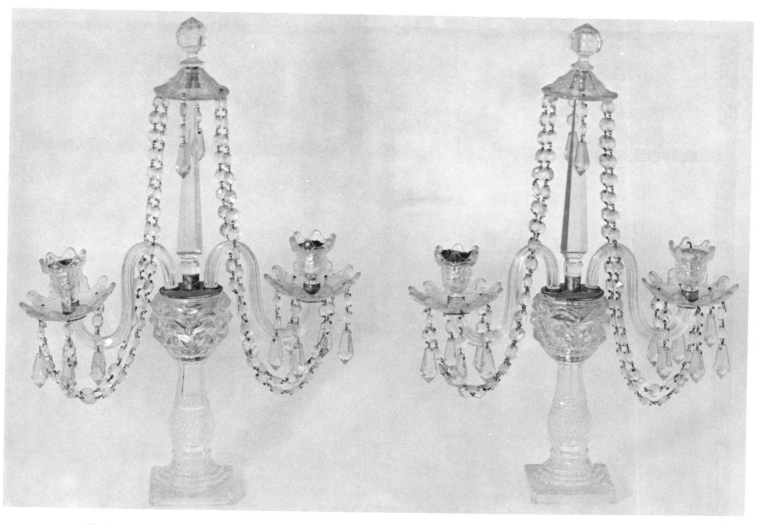

Pair of crystal candelabras, circa 1830,   pr. $500.00

a.–c. Pair tall Sandwich whale oil lamps with water-fall bases and etched fonts,
    circa 1840,   pr. $700.00
b. Lacy Sandwich tray (large), circa 1840, $290.00

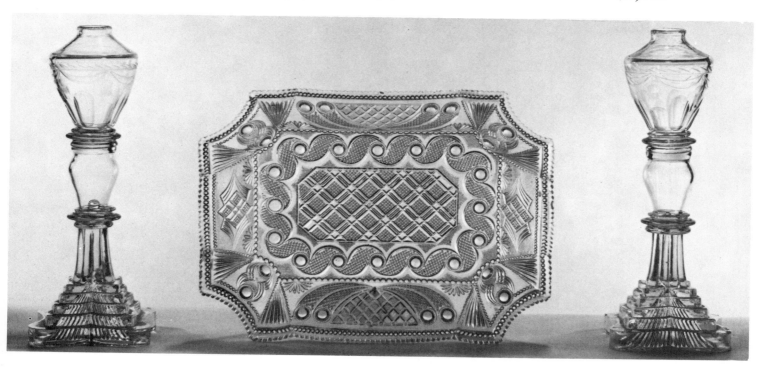

Bottle collection
TOP SHELF: *a.* $40.00   *b.* $45.00   *c.* $30.00   *d.* $60.00   *e.* $70.00
CENTER SHELF: *a.* $90.00   *b.* $80.00   *c.* $45.00   *d.* 70.00   *e.* $60.00   *f.* $40.00
BOTTOM SHELF: *a.* $80.00   *b.* $90.00   *c.* $120.00   *d.* $130.00   *e.* $80.00.   *f.* $65.00
g. $60.00

Collection of Amberina:
Small Pitcher $50.00 *Vase with applied glass* $160.00 *Pitcher* $260.00 *Shade*
$50.00 *Bottle* $120.00 *Carafe* $100.00 *Hat (not Amberina)* $35.00 *Fluted Plate*
$40.00 *Toothpick holder* $170.00 *Wine* $40.00 *Folded edge dish or tray* $130.00
Stoddard Hat $250.00 *Toothpick holder* $100.00 *Three punch cups,* each $120.00
Tall vase $130.00 *Vase (Left Front)* $50.00 *Five punch cups,* each $45.00

Battersea boxes, enamel on copper, circa 1760–80
FIRST ROW : a. $80.00 b. $75.00 c. $80.00 d. $90.00 e. $100.00
SECOND ROW : a. $85.00 b. $200.00 c. $160.00 d. $80.00 e. $175.00
THIRD ROW : a. $85.00 b. $250.00 c. $80.00 d. $75.00 e. $85.00

Group of paper weights. Center illustration shows Millville rose, $600.00; others
ranged in price from $130.00 to $300.00, circa 1860–80

Collection of Miniatures (Note: Eyeglasses show proportion)
Candlesticks pr. $75.00   *Piano* $85.00   *Ship* $45.00   *Teapot* $65.00   *Candle-*
sticks pr. $90.00   *Seven spoons* $70.00   *Silver teaset* $110.00

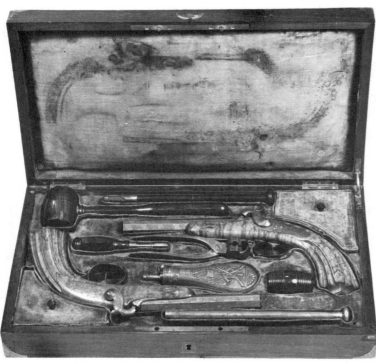

Very fine pair dueling pistols with burl
walnut handles, with all accessories
$900.00

Foot scraper, circa 1760

$150.00

Collection of fire buckets
a. $120.00   b. $110.00   c. $250.00   d. $120.00   e. $375.00

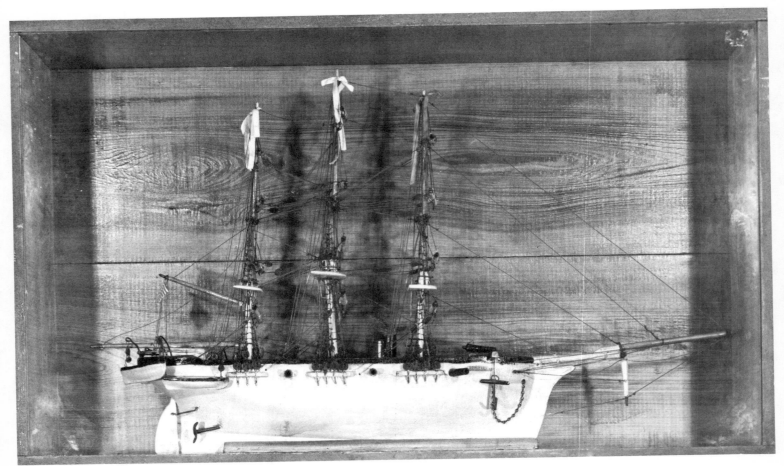

Encased ship model, circa 1830, $750.00

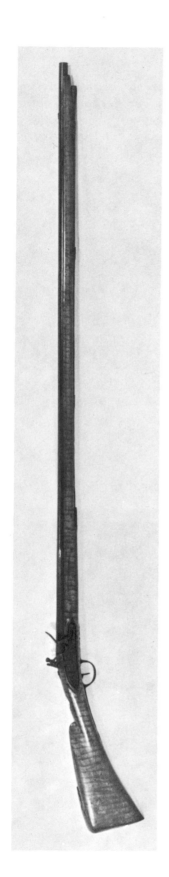

Early wire bird cage, circa 1830
$530.00

*Hudson Valley flint lock fowling piece
with curly maple stock*
$1,550.00

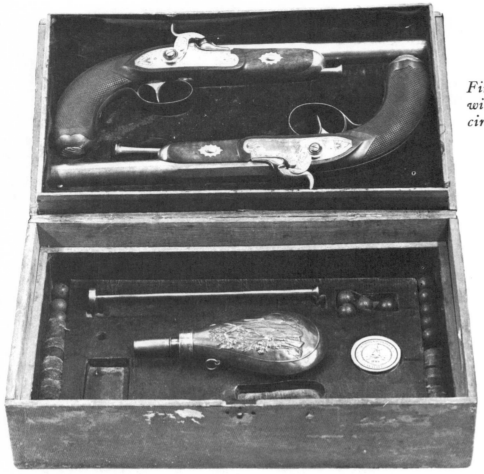

*Fine pair of encased dueling pistols
with powder flask and tools,
circa 1800–20*

$850.00

*Colt pistol in original
box with parts and tools,
circa 1810–30*
$1,050.00

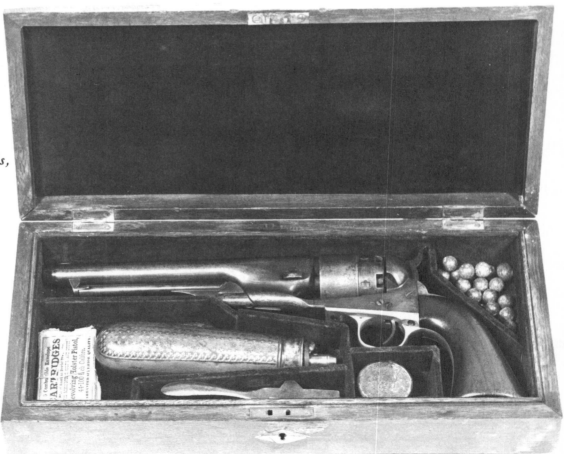

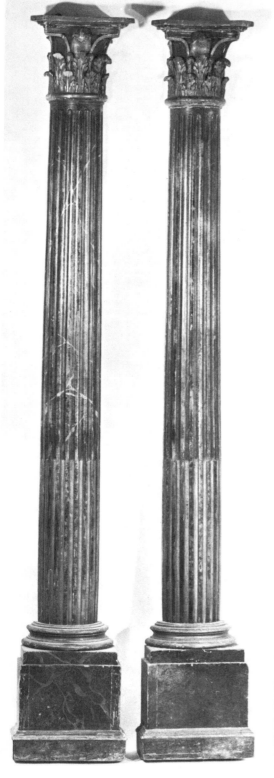

Pair decorative columns seven feet high

pr. $250.00

Brass pair scales, circa 1780 $525.00
   a. Bell $30.00

a. Bronze buckets   each $120.00
b. Geese   each $140.00

Ship Chronometer, made in New York
$600.00

Oriental vases
a. Pair bronze vases pr. $400.00   *b. Cloisonne vase on stand* $1,050.00   *c. Pair*
bronze vases pr. $250.00

a. *Covered Satsuma urns,*   pr. $1,250.00
b. *Satsuma figurine,* $ 900.00
c. *Teakwood stands with marble inserts* $300.00, $350.00, $300.00

Oriental gong on stand

$450.00

Music box with marquetry inlay, by Chevob and Company (Late Baker-Troll and Company) plays metal disks

$1,500.00

Oriental teakwood screen with Canton China inset 28″ high

$750.00

Collection of fire Americana, circa 1840
a. Hat $70.00   *b. Hat* $60.00   *c. Silver engraved trumpet* $300.00   *d. Hat* $70.00
Insurance Company Marks   *a.* $50.00   *b.* $80.00   *c.* $90.00